If The Sun, Moon and Stars Could Talk

Ameenah Rasheedah

Milligan Books   California

Published and Distributed by:
Milligan Books, Inc.

Cover Design by
Clint D. Johnson/Artistiq Reign Creations

Formatting by
Alpha Desktop Publishing

First Printing, April 2005
10987654321

ISBN 0-9764690-1-4

Milligan Books, Inc.
1425 W. Manchester Ave., Suite C
Los Angeles, California 90047
www.milliganbooks.com
(323) 750-3592

Dedication

To my family and friends. May this book be informative as well as an inspiration to you and your life's endeavors.

Table of Contents

Acknowledgments

Special thanks to my family, friends and everyone, who supported the efforts of this book and in making it a success.

Special thanks to my publisher, Dr. Rosie Milligan for helping me make this book a reality.

Preface

I want to make it very clear to those who read my autobiography, that this is the story of my life. I am writing this mostly for my family and friends, so that they will get to know something about my life. If I live to complete this book, upon my demise, I want it to go to Edward Vaugh. Edward is presently in the process of opening a bookstore and a museum in Dothan, Alabama (Birmingham). He has promised me he will keep all my papers and my life story in his bookstore. His location is conveniently located near my relatives who may wish to read my book. I am donating all my books to his bookstore. All my picture albums will also be in his store. I hope and pray after I am no longer in this world; some of my family members in the future generation will get to know something about my life. I hope and pray life for them will be better. I don't mean in material things, but in knowledge about themselves as sons and daughters of former slaves. The public school system will never teach Blacks about themselves in the schools.

I have spent a lifetime reading books about the legacy of black people in this racist society, and we have to accept the truth about what has happened to our people in America. I like what Carter Hanna said about this subject in his *Literary Gems* position statement, "When we read books written by African Americans, we get more than a story. We get the wisdom of those who have journeyed before us and a glimpse of life extracted from the experiences of those who are journeying with us today. Whether the story is resourceful, cunning, innovative, or a tale of defeat or triumph, they offer insight, survival skills and techniques to deal with life and its perplexities. If we are in search of ways to gain greater love for our fellow humans, knowledge of self and who we are as a people is necessary. True knowledge of our past and the truth about our present is a blue print for our liberation. In our literary tradition we find thoughts and ideas to empower our people to take charge of their "destiny."

INTRODUCTION

I think the most difficult task I have ever undertaken is to try and write my life story. Where shall I start, and when will it end? That was an understatement because I believe life goes on and on, only death brings it to an end, as we know it. I believe that there is another dimension or another stage where our ancestors, with the help of God, are waiting to help us into the second phase of our spiritual existence. When I made a decision to write my life story, I promised myself that I would be honest and truthful; I also made a decision not to go into any intimate details of my life because I don't believe it would serve any purpose for myself, or others to reveal details of intimate personal experiences. I have had good and bad relationships and I learned something from each of them. I have also made some mistakes in my life, mostly due to ignorance. I don't believe my Creator will hold me responsible for mistakes I made due to a lack of knowledge of my environment and myself. I hope this book will give my family and friends some insight into my life and a better under-standing of who I am. I suffered a lot of pain at the hands of my family and friends, because I was often misunderstood. I am not feeling sorry for myself, but rather for my family and friends, because it was their lack of knowledge of themselves that created all kinds of social problems for them.

I was born Lovine Loyd (the name on my birth certificate), in Decatur, Alabama. My father named me Lorine. After I became an adult, I changed my name to "Loraine" because I liked the sound of it. I changed my name to Ameenah Rasheedah on May 24, 1977, in Probate Court in the state of Michigan. I didn't want to spend the rest of my life carrying a slave name. My family got very angry with me for changing my name. My Father named me Lorine, and my family felt that I had disrespected my father. I realize I cannot change the legacy of my birth, but I do not have to be reminded everyday of my slave culture. When I changed my name, it didn't have anything to do with my father. I didn't realize it would create so many problems for me. I believe when an individual is called by their name, it has the same principle as saying a prayer. When we say a prayer, most people believe that an invisible God hears it, and that God is a positive force in the universal atmosphere.

My slave name is a word, and when I am called by that name it goes out into the universal atmosphere. I believe that name is negative, and most things that are negative come back to you.

Prior to my birth my mother had two boys, who are now deceased. I was born in 1932; the year Roosevelt was elected president of the United States. Because of the depression, life was difficult for my family. Both Black and White folks had a hard time.

I waited so long to write my life story because I knew it would be very painful to relive the segregation, lynching and Jim Crow laws, and the recollection of how we just managed to survive. Decatur is a small town located in North Alabama. During the depression Decatur had a population of about 38,000. My mother gave birth to eight children, but one child was a stillbirth. I remember as a child hearing my father and grandmother making burial arrangements for the child. My oldest brother was born March 28, 1928, and my next brother was born December 4, 1929. My mother said she had a difficult pregnancy with my second brother. She said he kicked her so hard she wanted to take a knife and cut him out of her stomach. When my mother made that statement, I remembered the pain I felt. She then explained why she made the statement. She said she knew my brother was kicking her because he was hungry; she was not getting enough food to eat. Although she knew my father was doing his best to feed his family, there was never enough food.

My father did not have a full-time job; he was a barber and he cut hair at home, charging about 25 cents a head. He eventually found a regular job working at the brickyard. He continued to cut hair on the weekend at home. Some years later he worked on the weekend in a barber shop located on Vine Street. He also hunted small game and spent a lot of time fishing.

There were days when we didn't have any food. My father would go fishing early in the morning and my mother would bake biscuits. Before we could eat, we had to wait for my father to bring the fish home. He worked hard to support his family, but I never remember him owing a suit. My mother said my father eventually had to take her to live with his mother so that she would have enough food. When my brother was born, he had very bad epilepsy seizures, and was under-weight. He was also short in stature and never weighed more than 130 pounds. Whereas, my oldest brother was 6 feet tall and his average weight was 170 to 180 pounds. My mother said by the time I was born, their financial situation was a little better. I always knew something was wrong with my brother because he had a very difficult time in school. He never learned to read or write. When I started school, he was in the second grade. He had to repeat the second grade, and by the time I got to the third grade he was still in the third grade.

I remember trying to help him with his lessons and keep up with my own. I also remember crying when our classmates called him dumb.

THE WHIPPING I WILL NEVER FORGET

I will never forget the whipping my bother and I suffered at the hand of our third grade teacher, Mrs. Thomas. She displayed a heinous attitude toward my brother and was a mean spirited individual. I can't remember what happened that caused her to whip my brother, but I ran up to her and tried to pull the belt from her, and I was crying and begging her to stop beating my brother. At that point she started beating both of us. Our backs were bloody and my blouse was in strings.

I am 72 years old and even today I can still feel that whipping. Every time she would strike my small back with that belt, it felt as if my breath had left my body. My brother and I had to hold on to each other just to make it home. When my parents and oldest brother saw how this teacher had beaten us, they cried and became very angry. By the time my parents made it to the school, my oldest brother had already been there. The authority prevented my parents from seeing the teacher because my oldest brother had attempted to do her bodily harm. I believe they went back to the school the following day. But after that incident, I don't ever remember seeing Mrs. Thomas again. This incident was often discussed in my home. My father often said he didn't understand how any adult would beat a child like this teacher beat us.

When my brother and I reached 7th grade, he could not keep up with his studies and I did not have the opportunity to keep helping him. He just didn't want to go to school anymore, and eventually just dropped out.

MY BROTHER AND HIS FRIEND

My brother and his friend spent most of their time gathering scrap iron to sell to the government for war weapons. I think this was in 1941 or 1942 because it was during the time of World War II. My brother began drinking at a very early age and eventually became an alcoholic. He passed away at the age of 56. Even today, many black men turn to drugs and alcohol just to kill the pain of trying to survive in this racist and hostile society.

The situation with my oldest brother was completely different. He did very well in school, and was considered a very smart child. I remember when he was about 12 or 13 years old, he drew a picture of a dollar bill. When the neighbors came to our house to get their haircut, my father bragged about how talented my brother was, and kept the picture on the wall for all to see. My brother used to make sketches of them while they waited to get a hair cut. My father was so proud of him. I think it was also during this period when my brother asked my father to get him a chemistry set for Christmas. He got the chemistry set and blew up our chicken house. He also used to keep boxes of books, and we never knew where he got those books.

My brother's teachers often complained to my father about his behavior. When my father confronted him, he would tell my father that the teachers would get angry with him because they could not answer his questions. We all looked up to my brother because he was very smart. He was also another victim of this racist environment, but he had some very serious disciplinary problems. At the age of 14 he became rebellious and got in trouble for stealing, and committing other petty crimes. He was eventually sent to reform school. I believe this was the beginning of some problems that would remain with him for the rest of his life.

FAMILY SECRET

When my brother was sent to reform school, my father had to sign a consent form stating that my brother was incorrigible. I believe my father later regretted that decision because my brother was in and out of prison for the rest of his life. During this period a lot of things happened in our home that I was too young to understand. Some years later, I learned that my brother was gay and that it had been a well-kept secret in my family. I never heard it from my father or mother, and my brothers didn't tell me until after the death of my father.

When he came home from the reform school, my brother was exhibiting all the signs of homosexuality; all his mannerism pointed toward homosexuality. He would sew his shirts up in the side to make them fit, and was always doing something to his hair. I didn't understand why he was doing those things, but I now realize why my father would use the expression "I wish Junior would change his behavior." I can remember only one gay person in my hometown. During that time homosexuals were called sissies. I don't remember any females living that lifestyle.

My brother went into the army and was only there for a short period of time. Something happened to my brother while he was in the army and he was discharged. Even today I don't know what happened to my brother and why two soldiers had to bring him home. My brother was very handsome and people used to tell my parents that he was the best looking child they had. I realize now my father may have felt responsible for my brother's lifestyle. He always said he was sorry he signed the consent form that gave the authorities permission to send my brother to reform school. I believe my brother was introduced to that lifestyle while in prison.

MY BROTHER WAS MURDERED

My brother was murdered in a hotel room in California. A maid discovered his decomposed body. The police didn't know how long he had been dead. He had been shot in the head, and that was in 1980. He had been dead several years before we learned of his death. My mother asked about him before she died and I decided to try and locate him. I wrote the Social Security Administration and they answered my letter and informed me that according to their records he had died in Los Angeles, California. They didn't have the correct date of his death, but stated that I could write the coroner's office for additional information. I wrote them and they sent me a record of the autopsy report. When I received the news about the death of my brother, it was very painful because the last time I saw him I said very hateful things to him.

When I look back at the incident, I was still angry with him for not attending my father's funeral, and I never had the opportunity to tell him I was sorry about the things I said to him. And I never got to really know him. We never had an opportunity to spend any time together. When I read the autopsy report and the statements made by the detectives, I knew to them my brother was "just another dead nigger." When I think about his life I can understand why he stayed away from his family. Most Black Americans have some very serious problems accepting homosexuality. Too many of our brothers and sisters have been totally destroyed by family members and neighbors in their environment because they were gay.

I think this is very sad. This is the result of some backward religious teaching. Regardless of an individual's sexual orientation, we don't have the right to make critical judgment about them because of what they do in their bedroom. Their sex life doesn't make them a good or bad person.

CONFLICT BETWEEN MY MOTHER AND MY PATERNAL GRANDMOTHR

I think I was about four or five years old when I had my first recollection of myself as a human spirit. It seemed as if I had been awaken from a deep sleep, and I saw my mother nursing her baby. I saw my father for the first time. During this time my grandmother was living with us (my father's mother). She was a domestic worker (for an old white family). I spent a lot of time with my grandmother. Sometimes she would take me to work with her, and I would help her clean house and cook. She taught me everything I know about housekeeping. My father was my grandmother's only child, and my grandmother was very protective of him. That created problems between my mother and my grandmother. My grandmother didn't think my mother was good enough for my father. I often heard my grandmother say she wished my father had never married my mother.

MY MATERNAL GRANDMOTHER'S CAPTURE IN AFRICA

My grandmother from my mother's side of the family lived in Athens, Alabama, a small town about 12 miles from Decatur. I don't remember much about her because she died in 1938. I was six years old, but I still can remember a few things about her. All of my grandparents were children during slavery. My mother's grandmother was brought to this country on a slave ship. She was 18 years old when she arrived with her mother and one brother. My mother said her grandmother often talked about her life in Africa, and how they were taken out of Africa. Martha Beck was her slave name. My great-grandmother remembered the name she used in Africa, but my mother said she never mentioned her name. She said that slaves were never allowed to mention the names they used in Africa.

My grandmother told my mother the story about her trip to America. She said that she and her brother went with their mother to visit neighbors in another village, when they arrived they saw their neighbors getting in a wagon with some white men. They got in the wagon also, thinking they were going to pick berries, and the next thing they knew the white men held guns on them until they arrived at the ship. My great grandmother couldn't remember how many months they were on the ship. When they finally arrived in the United States, they were separated and sold on the slave block. My great grandmother said she eventually heard that her brother was on a plantation nearby; but she never knew what happened to her mother.

Her father and other family members were left in Africa. My mother said that she believes her grandmother was from West Africa, but she couldn't remember the name of the country.

The horrendous institution of slavery didn't just destroy African families in this country, but it also destroyed families left in Africa. My mother said her grandmother couldn't remember much about her family left in Africa, but a strange thing happened, on her deathbed; she started speaking in her native language.

A TASTE OF SLAVERY

When I was a young girl, I believe slavery was still practiced in some parts of the South. I remember an incident where my oldest bother and a neighbor were digging under the house for fishing worms. Floyd felt something pull on his fork; he reached under the house and pulled out a Black woman. She had chains on her legs and she was wearing flour sacks for clothes. Apparently she had been hiding under the house for sometime. I remember how the dirt was caked on her skin. I believe my father and some neighbors tried to remove the chains. I also believe the police were involved in removing the chains. When this incident happened, I think I was about six or seven years old. I remember my grandmother and some women from the community giving her a bath and some clothes. I believe they did everything they could to help her. I don't remember what happened to her. I do remember inquiring about the chains, but I never got a truthful answer. I believe my people were trying to forget about slavery.

During my early childhood I never heard anyone discussing slavery, and it wasn't taught in school. Sometimes we would sit around an old lady we called Mama Lilly, and she would talk about her life during slavery. I believe her mother and father were slaves.

THE VILLAGE CONCEPT

When I was in Africa, I spent about three months living in a village. I noticed all the children were disciplined by the elder women in the community. The young mothers could work and shop without worrying about their children. They didn't have to ask anyone to baby-sit their children, because they knew the elder women would take care of them. Mama Lilly still practiced some traditions that came from Africa. For example, all the children had to pass her house going to and from school.

Mama Lilly would sit on her porch and watch everything, and would whip any child in the neighborhood. I don't remember anyone ever confronting Mama Lilly about whipping his or her child. She would always bring the child home and tell the parent why she had disciplined the child, and then she would whip the child in front of the parent. I don't remember what happened, but she saw my brother do something and she brought him home and whipped him in front of my parents. I remember getting very angry with my parents. I felt it was wrong for them to let her whip him.

Mama Lilly had a small two-room house that sat across the alley in front of the churchyard. Mama Lilly had one son and one or two daughters. I don't remember much about her daughters, but the son was big Ed Brown, and he had a son that was called little Ed. He owned a barbershop located on Vine Street. Big Ed lived on my street, the next block from my house. We thought Mr. Brown was rich. He made his money from holding games and selling corn liquor in his home. He also had a big dance hall located in the back of his house. He had spent several years in prison, but he always managed to get out. He always kept big cars and on some Saturday nights he had a big dance. We would sit on our porch and watch the people going to the dance. Sometimes he had big name bands from the North to play for the dances.

MY FRIEND FROM CHILDHOOD

Mr. Brown had a granddaughter about my age. I don't believe Bernice's parents were married. After Bernice's father, Little Ed, died her grandfather played the role of a father to her, and he gave her everything she wanted. Bernice and I played together as children and were friends into our adult years.

When I was in grade school she had some kind of heart defect that caused her to have epileptic spells. Sometimes when we were walking home from school or playing, she might have one of those spells and we would have to take her home. Bernice's mother allowed her to start seeing boys at a very early age (at that time we called it courting). When I think back to that time, I recall that Bernice always appeared to behave like she was an adult. There was one incident that I will always remember. I was about 12 or 13 years old at the time. Bernice has some boys visiting her from Sheffield (a small town about 30 miles from Decatur). Mazie, a classmate of Bernice, was invited to her house to meet the boys, and Mazie talked me into going with her. We snuck out to Bernice's house and I don't think we would have been caught had it not been for the fact that it was before noon, which was the time we were supposed to be helping with the housework.

We were having a good time talking to the boys when we looked up the street and saw Mazie's mother and my mother walking toward the house. They whipped both of us in front of the boys. I can still feel the humiliation from that whipping. After I became an adult, I asked my mother about that incident. She said that they shamed us in front of the boys so that we wouldn't do it again.

MY FRIEND'S WEDDING

Bernice must have been about 14 or 15 when she became involved with Charles Johnson and they decided to get married. Charles was older than Bernice. Her grandfather gave her a big wedding, and I was one of her bridesmaids. That was the first and last time I ever participated in a wedding. My family could not afford to buy me a dress. I begged and cried because everyone was getting a new dress except me. Ruth, the young schoolteacher who lived across the street, remade one of her evening dresses for me. I will never forget that dress. It was pink and beautiful.

All the neighbors helped us get ready for the wedding. We spent a couple of weeks rehearsing for the wedding. The school music teacher, Mrs. Thompson, played the piano as we rehearsed the wedding march. Because the wedding was to be held at the dance hall, Big Ed had a problem finding a minister to perform the wedding ceremony.

On the day of the wedding, he was able to find a pastor from a small Church in the country, who chewed tobacco and stuttered, to perform the ceremony. The pastor wouldn't allow Mrs. Thompson to play the wedding march, but insisted we march to the hymn *"Nearer My God to Thee,"* which he sang. Each of us laughed as we marched down the isle; by the time we were all on stage, everyone was laughing. As I look back on those times, I can see that we had a lot of funny things happen to us. Those were some of the proudest Black people I have ever been around, and even today they are still proud. I could write a book entitled "The Black Bourgeoisie of Decatur, Alabama."

AFTER MY FATHER'S DEATH

After the death of my father, my mother and I would sit in her room and talk for hours during my visits. It was during this time that my mother began talking to me about the history of our family. I began taking notes because I wanted to remember everything she told me. This was in the early seventies and this was the first time my mother and I had ever been able to communicate with each other.

Between the ages of eight to ten, I was very nosy and would often listen in on adult conversations. I asked a lot of questions, but they never answered my questions truthfully. I believe the legacy of slavery was so damaging to the spirit of my people that they were like the walking dead. They also had to deal with ignorance, illiteracy and helplessness. In my lifetime, I have witnessed my people being systematically destroyed by whites with superiority attitudes, and it has affected me deeply.

FILLED WITH ANGER AND HATE

At one time I was very angry. I prayed to my Creator to please remove the hate and anger I had inside me. I now realize how difficult it is to harbor hate and anger; it seems to eat you up on the inside. It has never really left me. When I left this country, I began to feel a little better. The legal system of Jim Crow and white supremacy was very hard on us—everything was separated. We had to go in the back door of white folks homes, use separate water fountains, and we couldn't eat in white restaurants, although Black folks cooked the food. We could shop in "Woolworth" stores, but we couldn't eat at the counter. We could buy the clothes, but we couldn't try them on. We had separate facilities at the train and bus stations. Black folks had to buy food from a window in the back.

We had two movie theatres, and Black folks had to sit in the balcony. I think it was sometime in the mid-forties when a Black theatre was opened on Vine Street. I don't remember the year. I think it was 1945 or 1946. Vine Street was located in the heart of the Black community and they only showed Black movies. I remember the first Black movie I saw and how it really left an impression on me. It was a Black movie called "Cabin in the Sky." The images of the Black Actors and Actresses in that movie remained with me for a long time.

HOW THE BLACK COMMUNITY USED TO BE

The Black community was very close. We wouldn't go to white hospitals, and a very few white doctors would come into the Black Community. Most of the time we had a Black doctor in the community. I remember the first two Black doctors in the community. They were Dr. Cashin and Dr. Sharrard whom served the community well. Dr. Cashin looked like a white man. I remember how the streets were lined with Black folks during his funeral. All his relatives looked like white people. I am sure some of them were white. He was buried in a white cemetery. As a child, I wondered why they buried him in a white cemetery when we were not allowed to go into the cemetery.

Dr. Sharrard's name is on my birth certificate. He helped deliver me into the world. After his death I believe his family left Decatur. There have been times when we did not have a Black doctor. During those times, there were some very serious illnesses, and three children died who lived across the street from me. I don't think anyone really knew what was wrong with them. One of my brothers got sick from the same illness. My family was really worried because we thought he was also going to die.

My grandmother treated my brother with some leaves from trees and other home remedies. During that time family and neighbors would sit up all night with an individual who was seriously ill. I remember staying up all night. It was called "the death watch." The next morning my brother woke up and asked for some water.

I think it was in 1946 or 1947 when a young doctor and his wife moved to Decatur. He opened an office on Vine Street and built a home in the community. I stated when I first attempted to write my life story, that I knew it would be difficult. It has been very painful just trying to deal with events in my life and the lives of my family members. It has given me the opportunity to express my feelings for my people and the Europeans who created the problems for us. I still didn't experience some of the devastating effects of slavery that so many of my family members experienced. I can now understand why so many Black folks were ashamed to talk about their lives as sons and daughters of former slaves.

SOMETHING BAD
HAPPENED TO GRANDMOTHER

I remember an incident that happened to my grandmother. I was an adult before I learned the truth about what really happened. I think I was about seven or eight when it happened. My grandmother had to be in white folks home (at work) about 6:00 a.m. I remember my grandmother leaving home for work before sunrise.

My room was located in the back of the house next to the back porch. One morning I heard someone fall on the porch. I got out of bed and went to the back door and saw my grandmother lying on the porch. I got my father and oldest brother. They carried my grandmother to her room. Some neighbors came over and I heard them whispering; they were trying to keep us (the children) from hearing what they were discussing. I kept asking my father "what happened to big mama?" My father said my grandmother had been beaten and robbed by some white men. It was years later when my mother told me my grandmother had been robbed, beaten and raped by white men.

Even today I can still remember the pain and anguish on my father's face. What could he do? He couldn't go to the authorities and ask them to arrest the white men. It is sad knowing that even today the average Black American doesn't have any idea of what it is like to live in a hostile and racist environment. They don't want to feel the pain. So it's easy to pretend that they are o.k. We are being violated every day by the so-called law enforcement personnel; people who are being paid to protect us. All across this country, Black men are regularly being shot down by the so-called law enforcement (mostly by white policeman), and nothing is done about it. They call it justifiable homicide.

WILL I EVER HEAL FROM THE PAIN?

Conditions have not changed very much from the time I lived in the South. A Black man was lynched almost every day. Therefore, I know I will never heal; the anguish and pain of this racist system will be with me until I die.

We also have to accept capital punishment. In my opinion it is nothing but "legal lynching." In the last few years since they have been doing DNA testing, they have discovered that many Black men all across this Country have been wrong-fully imprisoned and executed. Most of them were framed by a white racist legal system. Even today when a white man wants to run for public office, he runs on the issues of "law and order," which is a code word for capital punishment. Life for Black men in this Country isn't worth anything. Life expectancy for Black men in this country is on the same level as men in the third world.

MY RELATIONSHIP WITH MY
MOTHER DURING EARLY CHILDHOOD

During my early childhood my relationship with my mother was not good. I believe she loved me but didn't really like me. Our relationship was never what I believe a mother and daughter's relationship should have been. I believe she preferred my brothers over me. She never showed any affection towards anyone except my father. I recall other mothers hugging, kissing, and singing to their babies. My mother never expressed those kinds of feelings.

During my early childhood we didn't have electricity; we used kerosene lamps. Prior to the birth of my sister, I slept in a room alone. I remember crying at night because I was afraid of the dark. My father would often sit in my room until I fell asleep. Occasionally my mother would sit with me. I would often tell my mother that I had a stomachache because that caused her to rub my stomach with turpentine. I just wanted to feel her touch.

I adopted other women in the neighborhood as my play mothers. Although my mother took good physical care of me, she did not give me the special attention and affection for which I longed.

After the death of my father, my mother told me that she didn't like my behavior and that she felt that I had been spoiled by my father, and that I antagonized my brothers. There is one incident that I will always remember. My mother asked me to wash my brothers clothes. At that time we washed clothes in a tin tub with washboards. I refused and told my mother that my brothers should wash their own clothes, and that I was tired of rubbing the skin off my hands on the washboards. My mother whipped me. I stilled refused. Both my grandmother and my oldest brother whipped me. I still refused to wash the clothes. Although this all took place in the morning, I sat on the back porch and cried until my father came home from work. As I expected, my father was very angry. He didn't say anything to my mother and grandmother, but he told my brother never to lay a hand on me again. My parents never discussed disciplinary issues in our presence.

WOMEN WHO INFLUENCED MY LIFE

There were many women in our neighborhood that greatly influenced my life. One of them was Ruth, a young schoolteacher, who lived directly across the street from us. She had twins by her first husband. He died at a very young age. She remarried and had several more children. I spent more time at her house than I did at home. I went to her house one day and found her crying. She told me that Herman, her husband, had left her and gone to Illinois. That really frightened me because that was the first time I had heard of parents separating. That night I had nightmares. When my father came into my room, the first thing I asked was whether he was going to leave us. I think I was a teenager when Ruth moved to Illinois and was reunited with her husband. I learned so much from Ruth.

There were a few houses on my street that were really just one and two room shacks with outhouses. One of the families, a mother and father, had two boys and three girls. I believe the mother did domestic work. I don't ever remember the father working; most of the time he was drunk. The two sons were also alcoholics. One of them was married to Corrine, another woman who influenced my life. They lived about five houses up the street from us and had about five or six children. She was very pretty and the youngest mother on our street. I loved Corrine because I could talk with her about anything. She seemed to have young ideas. Although she smoked cigarettes, Corrine always gave good advice and encouraged us to do the right thing. I learned a lot from her, and I could tell her things I could never tell my mother. Her husband was in the army. Whenever he came home, he asked us to leave his house. He was extremely jealous of his wife. I believe he thought we were delivering messages to her from other men. After he was discharged from the Army, he took a job driving for an old White family. The youngest sister left Decatur and went to Chicago. The middle sister was my sixth grade teacher, and my mother said that the oldest sister was in the room when I was born. I never remember her working. According to the neighborhood rumors, her boyfriend, George Reynolds, took care of her.

George Reynolds was one of the two morticians in town. He was also an alcoholic. I was always impressed with the family. The sisters wore beautiful clothes and their house always smelled like perfume. The oldest sister gave me my first hardback book to read. I think I was about eight or nine years old at the time. I always felt special with them, because I had been the only girl in the neighborhood for a long time. My father told me that they gave me a rocking chair for Christmas when I was about three years old and my brothers would push me off the porch when they rocked me. He said they pushed me off the porch so many times that he decided to get rid of the rocking chair. I don't believe either one of the sisters ever got married. This was a very strong family. When there was a crisis in the community, they were always helpful.

Another family that influenced my life was the Moselys. I believe they were one of the original families in Decatur. They owned three houses on my street. They lived in one of the houses and rented the other two out to relatives. A well sat between two of the houses and I remember seeing an older man and woman come out and draw water from the well. As I grew older I heard people talking about them. They appeared to be the only people living in the house. We called it "the Scary House," because of the rumors circulating about the couple. There were tall weeds and high hedges in the front of the house and tall bushes in the back. The neighborhood children would slip around the house and try to peep in the window, but we were never able to see inside because the shade was always down.

MY MOTHER SHARED
HER FEELINGS WITH ME

My father and mother were very close; they were married 47 years. After his death I asked my mother why she had problems expressing her feelings. My mother said that is the way it was in her family, they never exhibited any affection toward each other. I realize now that that behavior is a part of the legacy of slavery. Mothers learned not to show any affection toward their children because they knew that the child could be taken away from them at any time. I believe my mother suffered from some kind of emotional damage that was passed down from her mother and extended family.

SOME CONCLUSIONS I REACHED
AFTER TRAVELING TO AFRICA

I believe the spirit of the human form is the embodiment and the essence of our Creator. I also believe Blacks in America and Blacks born in Africa are more in tune with this concept than any race or group of people on this earth. I came to this conclusion from my travels in Africa and other parts of the world. I spent 14 days with "the Hebrew Israelites" in Israel. I realized at that time that our survival did not have anything to do with any kind of religious organization or religious orders. The Hebrew Israelites is a group of Black Americans who immigrated to Israel; they left this country in 1968. They first spent a couple of years in Liberia before eventually moving on to Israel. When they first arrived, the Israeli Government harassed them. They moved their community to a location in the desert; it's called Demone, Israel. Brother Ben Ammi led them out of the country to Israel; he is their spiritual leader.

The Israeli Government did not want any Black Americans living in Israel, and did everything possible to make their lives miserable. For example, sometimes the government would cut off the water, and for days the community would be without water. But, they were determined to remain in Israel and had to learn how to provide for themselves. They had to grow their own food and that was almost impossible because they lived in the desert. They had to make their own clothes, including their shoes. You would never know they ever lived in America. There is no drinking or smoking in the community and they are strict vegetarians and the children are well disciplined. I am convinced our environment has everything to do with Black American's behavior.

I HAVE MIXED FEELINGS ABOUT RELIGION

I have mixed feelings about religion, especially Christianity. Most of the older people in my community were deeply religious. My grandmother tried to live the life of a saint. I don't remember my parents ever confessing any kind of religion. However, my father read the Bible almost every day, and was considered a biblical scholar. But I don't ever remember him attending any church. I remember my father spending a lot of time discussing the Bible with the men in our neighborhood. My mother started attending church in her old age.

The religious practices during this time consisted of churches holding what was called a revival. The candidates would sit on the mourner's bench until they felt the Spirit. When that happened they would confess their sins and become a candidate for baptism. Most of the time the candidate would be a child or a teenager and occasionally it would be an adult. After they felt something they would use the expression "I got religion." I remember hearing some adults saying they had to tarry in the graveyard before they could find Jesus. I went to the mourner's bench but I never felt anything. As a child I was scared of religion. And I certainly was not going to the graveyard because I always felt the graveyard was for dead people. Years later I realized that during slavery the Christian faith was used as a part of our indoctrination into slavery. In some of our Black Churches this form of indoctrination is still practiced today.

My grandmother and some elder women had a prayer band. They held prayer meetings once a week. Prayer meetings rotated each week to a different member's home. There were three women who lived next door to us that I loved to hear pray. It seemed as if they arrived from nowhere, and helped organize the prayer band. To my young eyes they were the most beautiful women I had ever seen. There was something wrong with their feet. These women prayed with authority. I had never heard anyone pray like these women and they appeared to be so clean. Even today I often wonder about those women. I asked my mother several times if she could remember them, but she said no.

MY NEIGHBOR MRS. BROWN

I was about eleven or twelve when some new neighbors moved in next door. There were six children in my family and the neighbors had about seven or eight children. The mother, Mrs. Brown, came from a very large family, she had about eleven or twelve brothers and sisters. Their father was a preacher, and pastor of a church in the country. They had a car and on Saturday they would drive up to Decatur. Most Black folks who lived in rural counties had to come to town on Saturday to do their shopping, and get personal things done, like going to the beauty and barbershop.

I loved to spend time next door because they always had a house full of relatives. They were a little strange to me because I had never been around people who lived in rural counties. All of Mrs. Brown's brothers and sisters had long names. Sometimes they would have as many as six or seven names. When I asked, Mrs. Brown, she said everybody in her family carried the name of a dead relative. A lot of our people held on to some of our African traditions. When I went to Africa I noticed some families named their babies after dead relatives. Our people did some amazing things; they always found a way to survive.

I do not understand how any Black folks who worked in the fields lived to reach old age. Working in the fields was some of the hardest work I have ever experienced. I hated fieldwork and I often wondered why I never learned to pick cotton.

In the fall, Mrs. Brown, her children, my mother, my brothers and sister would all go to the fields to pick cotton in order to earn money to buy school clothes. I went to the fields on several occasions and the most cotton I could pick was seventeen pounds. My mother and Mrs. Brown could pick over three hundred pounds of cotton. My sister could pick over two hundred pounds. Everybody would tease me and make fun of me because I just could not pick cotton. They soon stopped taking me to the fields. I would baby-sit and cook for my mother. I did all the housework and my mother and brothers would give me money for keeping house.

Our new neighbors had a daughter about my age. We became very good friends, and I loved her. I discovered later that Maize was a master manipulator. On several occasions I got into trouble because she knew how to manipulate me. Mazie was very mature for her age. She had already begun having sexual encounters, and by the time she reached her fifteenth birthday she was pregnant and had to drop out of school. My father tried to keep me away from her, but I would sneak out of the house to be with her. I think it would have been impossible to keep me away from her, because I wanted to see her have her baby. My parents kept me in my room because they felt I was to young to witness the birth of a child.

LUCILLE AND ME

Another girl that I hung out with at that time was Lucille; we were in the same grade and our families were friends. We did everything together. We went to dances, basketball and football games together. We also had our share of teenage problems.

WHAT IT WAS LIKE LIVING IN THE SOUTH

When I lived in the south, it was like living in a different world; the exploitation of Blacks by way of Jim Crow laws and the lynching of Black men were everyday activities. I remember hearing people in my community discussing the Scottboro Boys. The second trial was held in my hometown. In the south during this period, the only way a Black man without money could escape the south, was to hop a freight train, we called them "hobos." Many passed through our neighborhood, and we shared our food and water with them, most of the time they only wanted a cool glass of water. Occasionally, they would linger in the community for a while, but in most cases they would keep moving to other parts of the country. As a child I often wondered where they came from.

I think before I go any further I should give some information about the Scottsboro boys. On March 25, 1931, there were a number of boys, Blacks and whites, and two white girls, all hitching a ride on a freight train traveling from Chattanooga to Memphis. Near Stevenson, Alabama, a fight ensued among the Blacks and whites, and the five white boys were thrown from the train. The white boys told the towns people of Stevenson that the Black boys were riding the train with two white girls. When the train arrived in Paint Rock, Alabama, an angry mob was waiting. Most of the Black boys got away, but nine were captured. All nine were charged with rape of the two white girls, they became known as the "Scottsboro Boys." They were all teenagers; the youngest was only 13-years-old. The testimony of the two white girls claiming they had been raped was enough evidence for the all white southern jury to condemned eight of the Blacks to death. Mass demonstrations were held in major cities across the country and the Supreme Court ordered a new trial on November 7, 1932. The second trial was held in my hometown, Decatur, Alabama. Most of the Scottsboro boys remained in prison for years.

MY LIFE WITH SAM AND RED

I think I was between the age of 15 or 16 when I was introduced to Sam Bankston. When he first arrived in Decatur all the girls seem to be in love with him. His first cousin introduced me to him. Although he was a little older, to my young eyes he was the most handsome man I had ever seen. He had just came home from the Navy and was staying with his cousin. When he walked into his cousin's living room, I was playing some records by Billy Holiday. His cousin was a young schoolteacher who was getting married, and had asked me to pick out some records for the reception. All of his family lived in Decatur (his sister still lives in Decatur). Sam was a rebel, he didn't play by anybody's rules, and he never had a job but kept big rolls of money. Everyone called Sam "a hustler."

I didn't have my father's permission to have a boy-friend, but I would sneak out to see Sam. When I look back on my life, I can see that everyone who touched my life, whether it was positive or negative, had some kind of influence on me as an adult. I remember Sam talking about how much he hated white folks, and how they treated the Black soldiers. He said that he would never work for them; he earned his living by gambling and making corn liquor in Decatur, which was in

Morgan County, a dry county. Sam's parents were deceased, and an aunt raised him and his sister. Sam took care of his sister and paid her way through college (she is presently a retired schoolteacher). His aunt was also in the educational system. She placed teachers in county schools. Everyone in the community had a lot of respect for his family.

Sam and his friends were very popular in the neighborhood. I remember several incidents where Sam and his friends united to protect someone in the community. There was one incident that I will never forget; it involved a young man name Thomas Russell. We called him Red Russell, because he was tall and had light skin. At that time most people in the South with light skin were called "high yellow." Everybody hung out on Vine Street (Black bottom). I lived in the next block over from Vine Street. Some white people owned a cafe on Vine Street, a husband and wife team (Rednecks). I believe the white man caught Red with his wife. The wife hollered rape, but, everybody knew Red Russell and the woman had been going together for months. I can't remember the specific details. Everyone was talking about the incident, and everyone was worried about Red Russell. Everyone knew that he would be lynched if he was captured. We knew he got away, but very few people knew where he was hiding.

Early the next morning, Sam asked me to go riding with him; he didn't tell me where we were going. There were three other people in the car. The driver was Walter Gaines, Sam's best friend, and the other men were Forest Whitfield, and, I believe, Walter's cousin. I didn't have any idea where we were going. I later discovered they were trying to help Red Russell get out of town.

RED WAS RUNNING FOR HIS LIFE

We first drove to the west side of town where Red was

supposed to be hiding in a barn owned by Sam's uncle. When we arrived at the bridge that crossed over into West Decatur, the police was there, and would not allow us to cross the bridge. They didn't have any problems with us walking across the bridge, but no one could drive their car across. One of the brothers walked across the bridge into West Decatur, and discovered the police didn't find Red. We knew we had to find a way to notify Red of the new pick up location. We didn't have the use of telephones, and the only way we could communicate was by word of mouth. Even today I don't know how they got word to Red where we would pick him up. We finally picked him up, and got on the highway that would take us into Mississippi. We drove for about ten miles, and stopped near a cornfield. This was the first time I encountered a person who was running for his life. Red didn't look like a human being; he was cover in mud and didn't have on any shoes. He had lost his shoes while running in the woods.

We drove him to Mississippi where Sam brought him some clothes, and some Black folks invited us into their home, and prepared some food for the group. Later that afternoon we drove Red to Memphis, Tennessee. Red caught a train to Chicago. Red remained in Chicago for years, but he returned to Decatur prior to his death. All the young men in the car that day are now deceased. Sam eventually moved back to Chicago where he died in 1963.

When we picked Red up on the highway, he was laughing and joking about how he escaped from the police. He said that he was hanging on the outside of the window by his chin when the police officers came into the barn. I often wondered how Red could joke about his situation, but looking back on the situation, I realize now that we often laugh and joke to keep from crying.

WE MOVED TO ANNISTON

At the beginning of World War II, my father went to work for the government; He worked at the Huntsville Arsenal. He had been there for several years when they transferred him to Anniston, Alabama. I think this was either in 1949 or 1950. My youngest brother was born in 1948, and I think he was about a year old when my family moved to Anniston. I remained in Decatur with my grandmother. Prior to my family moving to Anniston, my father spent the weekend with my family and rented a room in Anniston. I was happy when they relocated because I could do anything I wanted; my grandmother could not control me. I started doing my classmates hair. I was good at it, and I had a lot of customers.

My grandmother worried about me because I became more involved with Sam Bankston. I also start hanging around with older women. Most of them were in their early twenties, and I was only about seventeen and still in school. By that time my best friend, Maize, moved to Cleveland, or I should say her mother sent her to Cleveland because she had a baby born out of wedlock. I think her baby was about a year old when she left Decatur. Please note: during this period it was customary for families to send their daughter out of town if they had a baby without being married. And in most cases the grandparents would raise the child. In my hometown we didn't have to many young girls getting pregnant. You could get a bad reputation and the so-call good girls wouldn't have anything to do with you.

Prior to my family moving to Anniston, my father rode to and from work with one of his co-workers. There were several men who rode with them; they did a lot of drinking. There was also a lot of drinking in my home, especially on Sunday when my father was cutting hair. My father was a very proud man and I believe he loved his family, especially my mother. But something happened when he was living in Anniston alone. The man who provided him with transportation shot him. I remember the evening we received the telegram, we were very worried about him because we didn't know how seriously he was injured. My grandmother was in her room when we told her what had happened; she told us my father was o.k. We didn't have a phone during this period. I do not believe anyone in the neighborhood had a telephone. My mother and I and my next older brother went to Anniston. When we arrived in Anniston, we went directly to the hospital. The facilities for Blacks were located in the basement of Anniston Memorial Hospital. My father were doing fine. I can't remember too much about the events around my father getting shot.

There is one thing about Black Folks, "they keep secrets." I heard some rumors that my father and his friend were involved with a woman. I don't remember my mother ever talking about what happened, and even today I don't know the details of why my father was shot. I only got bits and pieces, but never the complete story. There are so many things Blacks folks just didn't talk about. During the last years of my mother's life, she told me a lot of things about my family. However, she never talked about the personal relationship between she and my father.

A SAD YEAR FOR ME

The year of 1949 was a very sad year for me. My best friend, Maize, had moved to Cleveland, and my close friend, Lucille, moved in with her boyfriend. I felt very much alone. I started spending time with a young teacher we called "Penny," I cannot remember her Christian name. She was older than me. I can't say the relationship between Penny and I could be described as friendship. I don't remember the word friendship being used often in our community. I think this was because you choose your friends, and most Black folks came together during that time because our survival depended on our love for each other, first as human beings and second because we all had experienced the legacy of slavery. The South had its own culture.

Penny had her own car. During this period very few Black folks owned cars. Penny's boyfriend lived In Huntsville, and this gave us the opportunity to travel to Huntsville and other small towns in the surrounding areas. Liquor was sold legally in Huntsville, and they also had the American Legion and the VFW club, both of the clubs were operated and run by Black Veterans. I had another friend that I really looked up to. I called her Grady. She was the girlfriend of Forest, Sam's best friend. Grady was the only one who treated me like an adult, and even today we have remain friends.

I remember when Forest wanted to send Grady a message by me, I had never met her. Forest said I would hear her because when she walked, her bracelets jingled. I remember several events where Grady and I almost got into serious trouble. I can remember one incident as if it were just yesterday. Grady and I went to a house party in the country (rural counties). The people sold chitlins, fish, and chicken dinners, they also sold beer and corn liquor. These houses were mostly shacks, and the roads leading to the houses were so bad that we often had to push the car.

We found this little shack in the middle of a cornfield; the Black folks were having a good time dancing, eating and drinking. They were gambling in the back room. Red Russell was the only person there from Decatur. When he saw us he said he was glad to see us because he didn't have a ride back to Decatur. I think it was around midnight when a fight broke out in the back room. Red was fighting with three individuals. We all ran outside, but we couldn't find the car. Red had been cut and bleeding all over everything. We eventually found the car. But, we couldn't find the road and had to drive across a cornfield to get to the highway. Grady and I was scared because we didn't know how seriously Red was wounded.

We finally made it home. We often laughed about that incident. Grady and I had some good times together. Grady is presently living in Decatur. We keep in contact with each other. There is something that bothers me about some of my friends; they don't seem to remember things. Maybe it's just the result of growing old.

MY HEART WAS BROKEN

Penny's mother was a very good cook, and she threw a lot of parties. Her mother cooked all kinds of good food. Penny was overweight and very insecure, and had problems keeping a good relationship with her boyfriend. She made sure all her friends were involved with a brother who lived In Huntsville. Her boyfriend introduced us to brothers who also lived in Huntsville. Tom introduced me to one of his friends by the named of Grant Harris. He was a good-looking young man, but I wasn't impressed with him. He thought he was the best looking brother who ever walked on the Earth. I had stopped seeing Sam Bankston, because he had recently gotten married. It broke my heart when he got married. I soon stopped hanging out in Huntsville and became deeply involved with a brother who had recently moved to Decatur.

I made myself believed I was in love with Robert McVay, we went together for about six months. When he asked me to marry him, I said yes. I just wanted to show Sam Bankston I could also get married. Robert couldn't find a job and decided to go to Detroit where his brother and sister lived. He promised to send for me after he found a job. I think Robert told me he had found employment sometime in 1951.

I didn't realize Robert was lying about finding a job until I arrived in Detroit. He borrowed the money from his sister to send for me. I left for Detroit in November or December of 1952. I had just turned twenty. It was cold and snow was on the ground. I had never been in cold climate. Although it was difficult for me to adjust to the weather, I was happy because I thought I was in the land of freedom. I was in for a rude awakening. My life in the south was nothing compared to life in Detroit. My husband was living with his aunt when I arrived. We lived with her for about a month before we had to find another place to live; there were too many people living in that house.

MY LIFE IN DETROIT

We rented a room from an older woman who lived on Wiken Street, which was about a block from Hasting Street (Black Bottom). That was the street on which you could find all kind of activities and people, including hustlers, prostitutes, winos, and the number runners. Robert and I would walk to Hasting Street just to see the sights.

Sometimes we would walk up Hasting Street to Rev. C. L. Franklin's Church. His first Church was located on Hasting Street. They had good singing and preaching and there was always a large crowd in and outside of his Church. That's where I first heard Aretha Franklin sing; she was a little girl sitting on a box singing and playing the piano. Rev. Franklin built another Church on the West side of Detroit on Linwood, sometime in the early 60s. He was also active in the civil rights movement. Rev. Franklin and Aretha had a close relationship with Rev. Martin Luther King. I think it was in 1965-66 when Aretha and her Father sponsored a concert at Cobo Hall in honor of Rev. King. I went to the concert. I also remember an incident that happened at the Church. It was called the "New Bethel Incident." Rev. Franklin gave the RNA (Republic of

New Africa), permission to hold a meeting at his Church. There was a shootout between the police and some members. I believe a policeman was shot. I can't remember if the policeman was killed and I can't remember the year, but it was in the early 60s. The two brothers, accused of shooting the policeman, were not from Detroit; they were from Cleveland.

I was fascinated with Hasting Street and often went back there. During this period there wasn't too many hard drugs in the Black Community. I only met a couple of brothers who were addicted to heroin. I saw beautiful Black women standing on the street waiting to turn tricks with White men. Late at night you could always find long lines of white men waiting in their cars to turn tricks. The neighbors called my landlady "Pimp." When I think back to that time, I don't remember anybody ever calling her by her Christian name. I soon discovered that most of Pimp's roomers were prostitutes. They taught me a lot about my new environment. I saw pimps whip prostitutes with coat hangers. I will never forget how I felt when I saw a prostitute with cigarettes burns all over her body. She said that two White men had locked her in a room and burned her for hours with cigarettes. I witnessed the worse kind of abuse. When I look back at that time, it was like I was living in the twilight zone, and yet there were still some Black folks who tried to take care of each other. Some of them still had a value system based on doing the right thing.

The numbers racket was big in "Black Bottom." Most of the pimps and the number runners drove big cars, including some Black folks who had their own businesses. During this period Black folks or Jews either owned most of the businesses on Hasting Street. The people in the community trusted the "numbers man." Some Black folks who worked during the day would leave their door keys with the number runners so they could go into their house to get their number slips. I very seldom heard of a home being burglarized. On a few occasions a number's runner might get killed for not paying off a number bet, or sometimes it would be about a domestic depute. Most of the Black folks were from the South and they brought a lot of their Southern values to Detroit.

During the early fifties when the Eisenhower Administration was in power, Black folks were having a difficult time all across the Country. Robert didn't have a regular job, so he did odd jobs and washed cars to earn money. It was all we could do to pay rent. There were days when we didn't have food, and Pimp shared her food with me. Although I had experience doing hair, I was unable to get work in a beauty shop because I didn't have a license. In the State of Michigan a beauty operator is required to have a state license. I could not apply for a license because I had not completed the required beauty course.

A friend of my father owned a barber and beauty shop located on Hasting Street. Everybody called him GW. I never knew his Christian name. He hired me to work as a shampoo girl on Friday and Saturday in his beauty shop; I was not required to have a license to shampoo hair. It gave me the opportunity to make a small amount of money. When I look back, I now realize that GW was just giving me money. He was trying to help me because of his friendship with my father.

I went to visit Mrs. Simmons, another friend of the family, who lived on Pingree Street. She lived on the west side of Detroit. She didn't like the area in which we lived, and she didn't like Robert. Mrs. Simmons helped us rent a room from Mrs. Holmes, an older woman who lived across the street from her. Mrs. Holmes was a deeply religious woman; she didn't allow her roomers to drink alcohol or to use profanity in her home.

There were several young couples living in the home. Robert started drinking heavy and running the streets. There was a young sister named Annie who also rented a room from Mrs. Holmes. Annie was aware of the problems I was having with Robert and tried to help me. She was instrumental in helping me get part-time work at Pick Fort Shelby Hotel, a large downtown hotel where she worked as a maid. I only worked two or three days a week, except when they had a full house, then I worked full time for two or three weeks. Although the work was hard, I didn't mind, I was just happy to have a paycheck. Mrs. Holmes eventually asked us to move because she was tired of Robert's drinking.

We moved into a two-room apartment on Third Street, about three blocks west of Woodward Avenue. In 1954 I was able to secure a permanent position as chambermaid. I remember the year because the following year, 1955, Emmett Till was lynched in Mississippi. The Detroit Free Press ran his picture on the front page. I remember how shocked my co-workers were when they saw his picture. Everyone was talking about the tragedy. For many it was the first time they had actually seen how horribly the White man in the South treated the Black man. However, the picture did not surprise me because I was born and raised in the South and knew the barbaric practices of the southern White man.

In 1956 I became very ill. I was not accustomed to the climate up North and didn't know how to dress for the cold weather. My body began to ache all over and I had no idea what was wrong with me. I could not afford to go to the doctor and Medicaid was not available in those days. Robert took me to the emergency room because I had a high fever and he could not wake me up. I was in the emergency room for about 24 hours, but I never saw a doctor. I think a nurse gave me some medicine to bring my fever down. They told me they didn't have a bed, and they transferred me to another hospital. I don't believe it was really a hospital. Frankly, I believe they sent me to that place to die.

I was diagnosed as having pneumonia; I discovered later I had pleurisy (walking pneumonia). They didn't have any doctors or trained nurses on staff. The so-called nurses wore blue uniforms. When they transferred me to this facility they also transferred another Black woman who also had pneumonia. She was much older than I, and they put us in a room together. I had still not seen a doctor. When I asked about seeing a doctor, they told me to shut up and go back to bed. I remember the sister hollering and crying all night. She kept asking for her son.

Early the next morning I noticed she was real quiet. I went over to her bed to see about her; I discovered she was dead. I went out in the hall and told a woman she was dead. The female employee made me go back to bed.

Someone eventually came to the room and discovered she was dead. At that point I refused to stay in bed and told them I was not going back to bed until I saw a doctor. I sat in the hall all night, and the next day they brought in a doctor who gave me a shot and some medicine. But I was still very ill. After that death, I knew I had to fight for my life. I can't remember how long I stayed in that facility, but I went home without checking out. I knew I had to get away from that place because the undertaker was taking four or five dead people out of the facility everyday.

Robert only visited me once while I was hospitalized; he was still drinking and running the streets. I don't think I would have survived had it not been for June and Rosemary, a lesbian couple who lived across the hall from me. I was not aware of their lifestyle until Robert began calling them "bull-daggers," and told me to stay away from them. But I thank God for those sisters. They cooked for me and provided food for me when I didn't have any money. They continued to help me until I was able to make it on my own. They never tried to influence or draw me into their lifestyle. I became aware of the fact that homosexuality was a growing practice in the Black community. I remember discussing homosexuality with June and Rosemary. I assured them that I would never judge their lifestyle, even though I didn't understand it. They proved to be real friends when I needed them. I believe God sends people into our life for a purpose. And sometimes it is to save our life. Throughout the years I lived in Detroit, June, Rosemary, and I remained friends.

Regaining my strength was a slow process. I think the problems I was having with Robert added to my illness. I was living in a very stressful situation; even though I was ill, I knew I had to work in order to pay my rent and buy food. Robert was irresponsible and abusive. We fought a lot. During one of those fights, the neighbors called the police. We moved almost every other month; because we were not able to pay the rent.

Robert was involved in a car accident in 1957. I don't remember precisely what happened, but he came home one day and said we were leaving Detroit and moving to Louisville, Kentucky. I was unaware that the police was looking for him. When we arrived in Louisville, we moved in with Robert's uncle and his family. They had two children and his aunt was pregnant with a third child. After two months, Robert's uncle asked us to move and announced that I could stay, but Robert had to go. I left with Robert; we moved in with another aunt. She didn't have enough room for us, so we slept on the floor.

Robert's aunt helped us find a small, furnished apartment in back of a secondhand store; I will never forget that place, because everything there was rusty. Robert found some yellow paint and we painted everything in the apartment yellow. I started looking for employment right away. I finally found a job working for the University of Louisville. I worked as a bus girl in the dining room. When the students finished eating, we had to clean the tables. It was very hard work and we had to carry large trays.

Robert soon went back to his old lifestyle: drinking and running the streets. I think we had been in Louisville about six or seven months when I discovered that I was pregnant. I began having medical problems in the second or third month of my pregnancy. I didn't have the money to see a doctor. Robert's aunt took me to see her doctor. He told me that I would lose the baby if I didn't stop working. I was terrified. I felt that I couldn't stop working because I needed the money. One night I woke up covered in blood. I went to the hospital and had to have an emergency operation. I lost the baby. For the next few days I didn't care if I lived or died. The thought of the hospital bill weighed heavily on my shoulders. Someone from a charitable organization came to visit me. I was greatly relieved when she told me that the organization would pay the bill.

I think I stayed in the hospital for about ten days. When I was released, I had no place to go because we had been evicted from our apartment. Earnestine, a sister who lived next door to our apartment came to the hospital to visit me. She told me that Robert had not paid the rent and they had put all of our things in the street. Earnestine had taken most of my clothes and stored them on her back porch.

When I left the hospital, I was very weak and didn't have any idea what was going to happen to me. Earnestine lived in a small house with her husband and four children; the entire house only had three rooms, two bedrooms and a kitchen. She and her husband slept in the front room, and her four children slept in the second room. I will never forget that night. Earnestine let me rest in one of her children beds. She also fed me and let me spend the night. When I woke up the next morning, both of my ears had been bleeding. I was really frightened because I had always heard that when your ears bleed, death is near.

The next day I knew I had to look for a place to live. It was raining so hard I could barely see, and I was so weak I just managed to put one foot in front of the other. This was a very difficult time for me. I didn't have anyone to help me and I had no idea where Robert was. But I was determined not to go to Robert's relatives because I didn't like their attitude towards me. They were born again Christians, and treated you like dirt if you didn't accept their religious beliefs. I had to depend on strangers to help me. I had only been out of the hospital for one day, but I knew I had to go back to work because I had no means of support. The doctor told me I should stay off for at least six weeks.

I found an apartment at 1300 Walnut Street. The owners, Mr. and Mrs. Brown, had added a small apartment to the back of their house. I didn't have any money. When I explained my situation to Mrs. Brown, she rented me the small, furnished apartment. The apartment was built too close to the ground; it was damp and cold, but I was just thankful I had a place to lay my head. Earnestine and her husband helped me move in and I still had not seen or heard from Robert. As I look back on that time, I am amazed that I am still alive. I returned to work before the bandages were removed from my stomach; I didn't have a choice, because I had to pay my rent and buy food. Earnestine and Mrs. Brown fed me until I received a paycheck. I was fortunate because I could also eat free at work. During my first week back at work, some of my co-workers helped me in any way they could. They didn't make much money and most of them had families of their own.

One day as I was finishing up my work, one of my co-workers told me that I had blood on the front of my uniform. I went to the locker room and discovered that the bandage had come off my stomach, and the incision from the surgery was wide open, I could actually see my intestines. I was terrified. During this period they didn't have emergency services (like 911). I changed my clothes and went to the hospital. I informed the nurse at the front desk that I had an operation at the hospital about two weeks ago and my incision was open and I needed to see a doctor. She spoke with someone on the phone and came back and told me that they refused to let me see a doctor. I tried several times to explain my situation to her and even begged to see a doctor; they still refused to let me see one. When I left the hospital I had no idea what I would do.

I could barely walk; I was leaning forward and holding my stomach when a bus stopped in front of me. I was so weak I could not get on the bus. I will never forget the bus driver; he got off the bus and helped me to board it. On my way home from the bus stop, I stopped at a drug store and bought bandage tape, gauze, and a bottle of peroxide. I went home and removed my clothes and poured the peroxide on the incision and bandaged my stomach. I think I stayed off work a couple of days; I had to go back to work because Mr. Register, my supervisor, had threatened to fire me.

The incision on my stomach finally healed, and with the help of God I eventually got my strength back. I never did go back to the doctor. I was afraid, but I was determined to survive. I don't believe anyone can really understand or should underestimate the strength of the human spirit. I have experienced so many awful things in my life, some I will never write about or tell anyone, because no one would believe me. Black Americans have problems believing anything outside their personal experiences.

I made the mistake of letting Robert move back in with me. He started hanging around my job, and my supervisor warned me that I would be fired if I didn't stop him from coming to my job. Robert went to work and for a while everything was o.k. but it didn't last. He eventually went back to his old lifestyle.

I think it were sometime in 1958 or 59 when we decided to move back to Detroit. It was my idea to move back to Detroit because I didn't like Louisville; it was like living in the South. I think I found a job working in a women's clothing store, "Ray's Sportswear." A Jewish family owned the store, and they didn't like Black folks; but they hired Black folks because the store was located in the Black community. The manager of the store was also one of the owners. I first noticed her racist attitude when she called a janitor "nigger." When I went to him and asked why did he accept her abuse, he said he needed his job and he had a family.

This woman rode Black folks backs like they were mules. She would ask the Black salespersons to clean the counters, sweep the floor and wash windows. She asked several of us to wash the front windows. A couple of the girls went to get water for the windows, I didn't move. She asked me again and I told her I refuse to wash windows, I was hired as a salesperson and that she only asked the Black employees to wash the front windows. Of course that was the end of that job. After that I think I found a job working in a restaurant. After that, I lost track of the jobs I had because there has been so much turmoil in my life. I have tried to block out some of the bad times.

I think Robert went to jail sometime in 1958 or 1959, and I think it had something to do with an old warrant. At that time we had an apartment on Canfield off Woodward Avenue. When Robert got out of jail, I left him for good. I found an apartment on West Philadelphia.

After I lost my job, Robert's aunt told me a Black woman named Doris was looking for someone to help her write numbers and keep books. I went for an interview and she hired me. During that period Doris and her husband, Ben, were still together. I started writing the numbers by taking the books on the phone. She also had number runners; they picked up the number books. Doris was a number booker and she paid my rent and gave me a salary. She had access to an unlimited amount of money. This was the first time I has been involved with anyone in the numbers business. Doris was a fascinating woman. She kept large sums of money in her house. During that time I don't remember any Black folks writing checks. And I don't think they had invented the credit card. Doris had a beautiful home and spent a lot of money on clothes, furniture, and anything else she wanted. I had never heard of anyone paying five hundred dollars for a dress before; but everything Doris bought was expensive.

Every day large sums of money changed hands. I also discovered that Doris was relaying some of her business to a group of Italians who were involved in organized crime. I had been working for her about a year when she started giving me more and more responsibilities. I think I had been working about two years when Doris and Ben separated and she filed for divorce. Both of them had to move out of the house until the divorce was final.

While she was waiting for the court to make a decision about how the property would be divided, Doris moved in with me. She didn't like my apartment, so her boyfriend found us another apartment. We moved to 2903 Elmhurst Street, which was one block over from Linwood Avenue. We moved into apartment 209 and Diana Ross's father, Sam Ross, lived next door in 207. He and his wife had separated. He shared an apartment with Ken Goldsmith. I remember his children visiting him, but I don't remember ever seeing Diana. We were in that apartment approximately one year before Doris was able to move back into her house. She also bought a four family flat next door. She had her house renovated before she moved back in and I moved into one of the flats next door.

The other three flats were rented to a highly paid prostitute, a numbers man, and a shoplifter. I think this was in 1960 or1961 and Doris rented the apartments for three and four hundred dollars a month. At that time that was a lot of money to pay for a flat, and the tenants had to pay their own utilities. I didn't have to pay rent or utilities. All of Doris's tenants drove big Cadillacs or Lincoln Continentals.

I liked Lavato, the prostitute, who lived in the flat above me. She was older than I, but we became good friends. She was from Alabama. She taught me how to wear make-up and buy clothes. We traveled to Alabama together. Her family lived in Birmingham and my family lived about fifty miles north of Birmingham. She came from a good family. Her father was a minister. He didn't know his daughter was a prostitute; Lavato told her family she worked in a bank. Lavato and I remained friends throughout the years I lived in Detroit.

During this period I made a lot of money. It never occurred to me to save; I used my money to travel all over the country. I would also go home to visit my family and take them money and presents. I enjoyed hearing people tell me how good I looked in my expensive clothes. Eventually it dawned on me how ignorant I was about a lot of things; especially how Doris treated people. I think I had been working for Doris about a year when I started observing the way she treated her customers; these were the people who gave her their number books. If there were too many hits on one book, Doris manipulated the books in order to avoid a payoff. It was horrendous the way she treated her customers. Some of her customers would call and beg me to pay off the bet.

If I mentioned anything to Doris about the customer's problem, she became agitated and told me to stop talking to them. I begin to notice a lot of things she did that was frightening. On several occasions, she had someone beat up the customers who didn't pay her on time. I remember Doris, and this big Italian guy she called "Ike," laughing and joking about incidents that he reported to her. I could hear him tell her, "I got the job done." I remember another incident that nearly scared me to death. Doris said her former husband, Ben, had broken into her house and stolen her long mink coat. I knew this wasn't true because the housekeeper told me that Ben came to the house when Doris was out and took the coat stating that he bought it. When Doris discovered that he had taken the coat, she became very angry. I didn't understand why she was so angry because she had a three quarter length sable coat, a mink stole, and a chinchilla. She kept saying, "I'm going to have the bastard killed." I wasn't concerned about what she said until she got on the phone and actually tried to find someone to kill him.

I had met a woman who was a friend to both Doris and Ben (she was also in the numbers business). I phoned her and explained the situation to her. She got in contact with Ben and he left the coat with Lillian and went to California. Approximately three weeks later Ben called and thanked me for saving his life. Doris had put a contract out on his life. I heard from Ben occasionally when I lived in Detroit, but I never heard of his returning to Detroit.

I soon realized I was working for a very dangerous and mean woman. She didn't care about anything but money and all the things she could buy. I had never met anyone who loved money so much; it was like a "god" to her. There were times when we collected large sums of money and Doris didn't like the smell of it; she took the money to the basement and washed it. Doris always kept large sums of money in a chest drawers and hatboxes. I took the job with Doris because I wanted to earn a living. However, what I learned about her frightened me. I discovered that these people had a value system that I did not understand.

I think it was sometime in 1961 when I made a trip to the South. I had been keeping up with the civil rights movement in the newspapers. When I arrived in Alabama I could feel and smell the wind of change in the South. Everyone was talking about of Reverend Martin Luther King, Jr. After I returned home, Reverend King came to Detroit and led a big march. I participated in the march and felt real good about being involved. Doris didn't like it; she kept saying, "I don't understand what those niggers are marching for." I think it was during this period that Doris and I had a serious misunderstanding; she fired me for paying off a number book. She was out of town and this older couple's book hit for about a thousand dollars and I paid off the bet. Doris fired me because she said I should not have paid the bet. So, I found myself without a job or a place to live because I had been living in Doris' place. I moved into a motel temporarily just to get away from her.

MY POLITICAL ORIENTATION

I met David Robinson shortly after I lost my job and moved out of Doris's flat. It was in the early sixties when the unions held a political rally on Labor Day in front of the old city county building. The unions were very strong in Detroit. I met David at the Labor Day rally in downtown Detroit. He taught school in Highland Park, Michigan, and was recently divorced. David was born and raised in Mississippi. We were both from the South and had a lot in common. We talked about everything. I told him about my living situation and he offered to help me find a place to live. David phoned me the next day and we went to dinner. He told me about a friend who had a big house and was looking for a roomer. She had two small children and her husband had been killed the previous year.

I didn't realize Kay was White until David took me to meet her. I had mixed feelings about living with a White woman, but I soon discovered that Kay didn't have a racist bone in her body—we had a good relationship. David and Kay insisted that I enroll in Highland Park Community College. I found a job working in a bar at night. David and Kay began to teach me about living in this racist country. Kay and her husband met on the campus of Wayne State University; they were both involved in the political activities on campus. Kay had been married to a Palestinian and deeply involved in the Palestinian Liberation movement; for that reason, she believed that the CIA had had her husband killed.

Let me take this opportunity to express my views about the Palestinian cause. I remember reading about how the United Nations had made Israel a Jewish state, but I didn't think much about it until I met Kay. I also met a couple of her husband's relatives who had just come to this country. They constantly talked about how the Jews had taken their land; one of them was killed under suspicious circumstances. Kay and I attended his funeral. I will never forget how I felt when we returned to Kay's house. We went into the decedent's room, we noticed that he had taken the bed down and moved all the furniture to one side of the room. He had been sleeping on the floor, and on the wall was a Palestinian Liberation flag. For the first time in my life I realized that I had met a true Revolutionist.

Most Black folks seemed to believe that the Jewish people who are presently living in Israel are the descendants of the people who lived in Israel thousands of years ago, but most of the people living in Israel today had never been to Israel before the United Nations made it a Jewish state. After World

War II, the European countries didn't know what to do about the European Jewish situation. So they decided, through the United Nations, to create a Jewish state; they picked out several different countries, and finally narrowed it down to Israel. The Jews wanted it to be called Israel because they believed that they had a God given right to that country. Before the decision was made to make it a Jewish state, the European Jews were already claiming it as a Jewish state.

As early as 1938, more than five hundred Palestinians were killed by Jewish terrorists; throughout the 1940s, Jewish terrorists planted bombs in restaurants, hotels, homes, and schools in many Palestinian villages and cities, killing and wounding hundred of civilians. In 1948 when they finally made Israel a state, the Jews had already driven almost a million Palestinians from their homes.

During the War of 1967, Israel took almost all of the Palestinian's land. The United Nations passed a resolution that would have given the Gaza Strip back to the Palestinian; but that didn't mean anything to the Jews, they had already began building homes on the Gaza Strip. I believe the treatment of the Palestinians is just as bad as apartheid was in South Africa. In recent years the Palestinians' living conditions have become so deplorable they have just given up. In the past few years the Palestinians have tried to resist Israeli occupation, and the aftermath of poverty and hopelessness has forced a small minority to turn to suicide bombing. It is clear that the never-ending occupation of the Gaza Strip will always add to the ammunition for the Palestinian suicide bomber.

When I visited the Middle East I was appalled by the living conditions of the Palestinians; it was unbelievable, I felt so sorry for the Palestinians, and no one should be forced to live under such horrible conditions. Today the whole world watches as the Palestinians are being murdered, without mercy, by Israel and without any intervention from the World Communities. The Israelis have the most powerful army in the Middle East, and the Palestinians do not even have a standing army. This country provides billion of dollars to Israel to buy weapons, which are used to murder innocent Palestinians. The warmonger, Ariel Sharon, has the blood of thousands of Palestinians on his hands; most of them killed in refugee camps in Lebanon.

I am certain that some of my so-called friends will say that I am anti-Semitic. I have noticed that anyone who speaks out against the Jewish people is given that label. I am not concerned about what names I am called, but I must tell the truth as I see it. There were a couple of articles, one in the Washington Post and another in the Washington Times, that created a lot of controversy about a television series, *Horseman Without A Horse*, that was scheduled to begin showing in Egypt on their state run television station. Approximately two hundred Jewish activists demonstrated in front of the embassy to protest the series. The Israelis accused Egypt of being anti-Semitic. The actor and producer, Mohammed Sobhi, said that the Israelis began criticizing the series before it was shown on TV, because a small percent of the show is based on *Protocols of the Learned Elders of Zion*. I read this book about thirty years ago. It's ludicrous to say that the book is anti-Semitic; Jews wrote the book.

I believe it was sometimes in the sixties when they tried to get the book taken out of the Black book stores and it is difficult to find it in books stores today. I have read the book about four or five times and the last copy I purchased had to be ordered. When I first read the book I didn't want to believe it. It was obvious to me that the book was written for one purpose—Jewish world domination. A blind person can see the control the Jews have on the world, and anyone who has read that book can see that everything that is happening today has been well planned.

I reread *Protocols of the Learned Elders of Zion* recently and it is clear to me that what has been writtened has already happened or it is coming to pass.

To illustrate an example: the following excerpts are from the book, *Protocols of the Learned Elders of Zion.* Chapter IV. Page 136 text and Commentary of the Protocols themselves, little need be said in the way of introduction. Sergyei Nilus in Russia published the book in 1905. A copy of this is in the British Museum, bearing the date of its reception, August 10, 1906. All copies that were known to exist in Russia were destroyed by the Kerensky regime, and under his successors, the possession of a copy by anyone in Soviet land, was a crime sufficient to ensure the owner being shot on sight. This fact is in itself sufficient proof of the genuineness of the Protocols. The Jewish journals, of course, say that they are a forgery, leaving it to be understood that Professor Nilus, who embodied them in a work of his own, had concocted them for his own purposes. Mr. Henry Ford, in an interview published in the New York Work, February 17, 1921, put the case for Nilus tersely and convincingly thus, the only statement I care to make about the PROTOCOLS is that they fit in with what is going on. They are sixteen years old, and they have fitted the World situation up to this time. THEY FIT IT NOW."

Part 1. A selection of articles published by Mr. Henry Ford's paper *The Dearborn Independent*, in 1920. *"Here in the U.S. it is the fact of this remarkable minority—a spare Jewish ingredient of three percent in a nation of 110,000,000— attaining in 50 years a degree of control that would be impossible to a ten times larger group of any other race that creates the Jewish question here. Three percent of any other people would scarcely occasion comment, because we could not meet with a representative of them wherever we went in high places in the innermost secrecy of the councils of the big four at Versailles; In the supreme court; in the councils of the White House; in the vast dispositions of world finance—wherever there is power to get or use. Yet we meet the Jew everywhere in the upper circles, literally everywhere there is power. He has the brains, the initiative, the penetrative vision, which almost automatically project him to the top, and as a consequence he is more marked than any other race."*

Beginning another excerpt page 9, *"And that is where the Jewish question begins. It begins in very simple terms— how does the Jew so habitually and so resistlessly gravitate to the highest places? What puts him there? What does he do there? What does the fact of his being there mean to the world?"*

Excerpt from page 94 to enhance the dignity of religious dogmas the following commandments are given: *that the Jewish nation is the only nation selected by God, while all the remaining ones are contemptible and hateful. That all property of other nations belongs to the Jewish nation, which consequently is entitled to seize upon it without any scruples. That an orthodox Jew is not bound to observe principles of morality towards people of other nations, and on the contrary, he even ought to act against morality, if it were profitable for himself or for the interest of Jews in general; a Jew may rob a Goy (a Goy means unclean and is the disparaging name for non-Jew) he may cheat him over a bill, which should not be perceived by him."*

Beginning page 200, *"of the Protocols, when the King of Israel sets upon his sacred head the crown offered him by Europe he will become patriarch of the world. The indispensable victims offered by him in consequence of their suitability will never reach the number of victims offered in the course of centuries by the mania of magnificence, the emulation between the goy governments."*

I believe this book should be read by anyone who is seeking the truth.

I will return to my relationship with Kay, the school-teacher and my friend in the masters program at Wayne University. This was during the period when college students began to speak out and protest against the War in Vietnam. Kay was a member of an organization called "The National Priority Against the War in Vietnam." The group was made up primarily of professors and college students on Wayne's campus, most of them were Europeans. Kay talked me into joining the organization and we attended meetings and rallies all over the state. There were a few other Blacks involved in the organization. I understand now why I believe life is a process of learning and how important it is for us to associate with right-thinking people.

I think I was about eleven years old when I began reading the newspaper with my father. It was during the time of World War II; we would read the newspaper everyday. Although I didn't understand what the war was about, I enjoyed reading the newspaper with my father. It was from this experience that I developed the habit or reading the newspaper every day. During that time we subscribed to *The Decatur Daily*, but as I grew older I read many books about the war. I remember reading *The Rise and Fall of the Third Reich*. I had a little more knowledge about the Korean War. I think I first became aware of the War in Vietnam In 1961 or 1962. I became aware of it through an article in the *Detroit Free Press* about a monk who set himself on fire in an attempt to draw the attention of the public to the role of the American Government in the war in Vietnam.

Several other monks followed suit in New York as well as other states. They would pour gasoline on themselves, strike a match, and set themselves on fire. That was the first time I had ever heard of anyone giving his or her life for a "cause." I was aware of the fact that a group of Japanese pilots formed suicide missions during World War II; but I never gave it much thought.

After I met Kay and became involved in the protest against the war in Vietnam, I realized that what this government was doing to the Vietnam people was evil. There was so much going on during the early sixties, that it was difficult for me to know what was really going on in America and what America was all about. It soon became clear to me that everything Black folks had been taught was a lie. I made up my mind that I would learn the truth about slavery, the Civil War, and the role of American Imperialism. At that time I honestly believed that we could change this country; I realize now that was just a dream. The sole purpose of the American government is to keep Blacks and Whites ignorant and in denial. They will use religion, the churches, and all kinds of propaganda to control the masses.

WINGS OF REVOLUTION

I have just completed the first fifty handwritten pages of my life story. From the time I can remember, during the early forties and the late fifties, I have had the most difficult time trying to write about the sixties. I think that's because the sixties was a time of real change. Everything was new, there was a new way of thinking, a new way of living, and a new way of believing, everyone had something to say and everyone had something to give. Some of their ideas were good and some were bad; but there were some people willing to fight for their ideas. The wings of revolution were spreading all over the country. For the first time in my life I met people who were willing to fight for change.

In the South we knew the southern White man hated us. But it didn't take long for me to realize racism was buried deep in this country, not just against Black folks, but also against American Indians and other people of color. Institutional racism is practiced in the schools, hospitals, and in state and the federal government. Racism is even worse in private businesses because most white-collar jobs are not unionized. I began participating in some of the civil rights marches; I even went down South a couple of times. However, I decided not to go back because I could not deal with the non-violent concept. I was too angry because I had experienced the brutality of the southern White man. I knew in my heart that the non-violent concept would not work for me. If I had a confrontation with a White man, I would end up in jail for murder. I have tried all my life to avoid trouble. I saw jail as a cage; a human being locked up in a cage. Presently, more than half of the prison population is Black men. Something is wrong with this picture when Blacks constitute only about twelve percent of the American population.

I think when I first heard Malcolm X speak, it was sometime in 1963. Kay and I were in New York attending a rally. I remember stopping at a Black book store in Harlem and the brother who owned the store started talking to me about Malcolm X and encouraged me to go hear him speak. Since he was scheduled to speak on Lenex Avenue at 1:00 p.m. that day, I decided to attend. Malcolm was a tall good-looking man who appeared to be very angry. Although I felt that this brother was telling the truth, I wasn't ready for his teaching; because I was still "a Negro," and still in the process of trying to formulate my own ideology.

The Honorable Elijah Muhammad reprimanded Malcolm about the controversial statement he made regarding the death of President Kennedy. If I remember correctly, a lot of Black folks also got angry with Malcolm, but his popularity continued to grow among young Black brothers, especially those in the Black National Movement. The day of the Kennedy assassination, I saw more Black folks crying than White folks. I believe a lot of Black folks believed that this young White man would make some positive changes for them. This is unfortunately because we are still exhibiting the same behavior from slavery. I think the next time I heard Malcolm speak was in 1964 or 1965. He spoke at King Solomon Baptist Church. That night he made his most famous speech, "Message to the Grass Roots." I will never forget that night; the church was packed and Malcolm gave the best speech I have ever heard. I think it was after the riot in 1967 when Kay got a teaching position in Lansing. She decided to sell her house and move to Lansing. I found another place to live on Webb Street one block from Dexter Avenue, and three blocks from Linwood Avenue. I mentioned these two streets because a lot was happening on these streets at that time.

Edward Vaughan was the owner of the largest Black bookstore in Detroit; his store was located on Dexter Avenue. The Black Panthers were also involved in political activities on Dexter Avenue. I heard Jamil Abdullah Ai-Amin (H. Rap Brown) and Kuame Ture (Stokey Carmichael) speak several times on Dexter Avenue. The Muslim Mosque was located on Linwood Avenue. They also owned restaurants and several other businesses on Linwood Avenue. Reverend Albert Cleage's Black National Church (The Shrine of The Black Madonna) was also located on Linwood Avenue. Reverend C. L. Franklin's Church (Aretha Franklin's Father) was also located on Linwood Avenue.

Black Americans had just begun identifying with their African heritage and becoming more angry about the American system of injustice. I was still involved with David, and he was teaching at the University of Michigan. I will never forget the Sunday Malcolm X was assassinated; I saw brothers crying in the streets. I was expecting riots to break out because of the riots that occurred in Watts and other parts of the country.

I soon discovered the FBI and the police were trying to eliminate the Black Panthers off the face of the Earth. Every other week I would hear of the police killing a member of the Black Panther Party. I was asked to join the Black Panther Party; I attended a couple of meetings, but they were teaching their members to pick up the gun and I wasn't ready to go to jail—they scared me. I think David was made the director of the OEO (Office of Economic Opportunity) Program sometime in 1966. The main office was located in Wayne County. When they opened positions in Highland Park, David got me a job as community organizer. This was the first time in my life that I had a job that I enjoyed.

A Black sister was the director of my office. We became good friends and had a good working relationship. There were also four other sisters and four white hippies. The white hippies spent most of their time organizing and protesting against the "War In Vietnam." I also worked with a young Jewish guy who was a Peace Corp volunteer; he joined the Peace Corp to avoid going to Vietnam. We worked in the neighborhood—organizing people to participate in community activities. We also offered free legal services, food co-ops, and employment services. It was a good feeling to be in a position to help my people. I remember the first time we organized some people around a decision to be made by the city council. They were scheduled to vote on the issue the following month. On the day of the meeting, so many people attended they didn't have standing room. One of the council members said this was the first time that many people had shown up for a city council meeting. I believe that people can make a difference and affect positive changes in their community when they become involved.

As I grew older, I had a better understanding of my past, and myself but I still have problems understanding what the sixties was all about. It changed my life, and I am convinced that if I live to be a hundred years old, that it was my experiences of the sixties that has given me the strength to continue to search for new knowledge and spiritual realities. I think what I am really trying to say is that those experiences forced me to change. I came from among the dead. This is a difficult thing for me to say, but the truth is the truth. I believe the legacy of slavery and Jim Crow laws have left some of my people spiritually dead, and a lot of White folks are not only spiritually dead, but they are also in total denial about racism and white supremacy in this country.

I think it was after the death of Malcolm in 1965 or 1966 when I noticed a lot of Black Americans becoming more militant. I was still working part-time at the bar, and the brothers who came into the bar had started talking about killing White folks. During this period Black folks were being killed on a regular basis all across the country. I remember reading in the Black Panther paper how the FBI had framed and set up Black Panther members to be either jailed or killed.

When the riots broke out in 1967, I was still working part-time at the bar. I had never witnessed this kind of anger among Black folks, especially from brothers. And it scared me. I can't remember the exact day, but the riots broke out on a Sunday morning in June of 1967. I worked about three blocks from where the riots started. On the night that the riots began, a brother came into the bar and told us the police was in the process of raiding an after hour house on 12th Street, and there were rumors that a policeman had thrown a Black woman down some stairs. I knew the brother who ran the after hour house; his name was Billy Gaines; he often came into the bar.

When the bar closed, I usually went home by taxi or the owner, Ron, gave me a ride. On this particular night, Ron drove me home and we had to cross 12th Street to get to my house. As we passed, we noticed Black folks throwing rocks and bottles at the police. I didn't think too much about the incident. I had only been asleep three or four hours when Kay called and woke me up the next morning saying, "All hell has broken out and Detroit is burning."

During this period my youngest brother Chris was living in Detroit. He had recently been discharged from the army and didn't want to continue living in the South. I got him a room with Mrs. Holmes; she was still living on Pingree Street. The second day of the riot I spoke with him several times by phone and begged him not to go out because I was worried about him. The police and the National Guard had been called in and they were shooting Black brothers down in the streets like dogs. I think it was the following day that I received a phone call from Mrs. Holmes stating that Chris had been out all night and had not been home. I tried to find him, but the National Guards would not permit me to cross Woodward Avenue. I soon found out that Chris had been arrested. I was relieved—at least I knew he was still alive. I also felt that Chris would be safe from death or injury at the hands of the police and National Guards on the streets.

During this period I did not cook any meals at home. I had cooking facilities but I didn't take the time to cook. I ate all my meals in restaurants. I often ate at a Howard Johnson restaurant across the street. After they brought in the National Guards, I couldn't leave home, and I didn't want Kay to feel responsible for feeding me because she had two small children to take care of. I decided to go home. I made reservations for the next day; I remember how I felt on the plane when I looked down at Detroit. It looked like the whole city was burning. My father was very angry with me for leaving Chris in jail. I tried to convince him that Chris was better off in jail and that he would be safer in jail than on the streets. I don't remember how many days I remained in the South. But when I returned to Detroit it looked like the entire city had been burned. I got my brother out of jail and went back to work.

My office had been closed during the riot. I learned that there were more brothers killed than had been reported on the news. There were several incidents that were never mentioned in the newspapers or on TV. According to the newspapers about 44 people were killed in the riot. However, there were still a lot of people missing whose names were not included in the count. It was also during this period that a lot of Black folks protested against the war in Vietnam. We soon discovered that more Black soldiers were being killed in Vietnam than White soldiers. During this period all the White folks in my office were in the process of organizing for the March on Washington—it was in 1968. I will never forget the year because I had never attended a march this large. I don't ever remember that many people coming together at one time for anything.

There is another event that stands out in my mind; the 1968 Democratic Convention that was held in Chicago. Some of my White co-workers went to Chicago to participate in the protest demonstration. One of them suffered a broken arm at the hands of a Chicago policeman. A lot of the protesters were arrested, including some young Black brothers, one of whom was Bobby Seale. When they had his trial, I remember watching it on TV and the judge had this brother gagged and chained to a chair in the courtroom. I have some serious problems watching Black men in chains. I think it had something to do with my experience in the South. When I was a child I remember seeing Black men working on the chain gangs.

MARTIN LUTHER KING, JR. IS ASSASSINATED

I will never forget April 4th, 1968; that was the day Martin Luther King, Jr. was assassinated. I had stayed overnight at Kay's house in Lansing, Michigan. The night before his death, Reverend Martin Luther King, Jr. appeared in news briefs where he made his famous statement, "I Don't Fear Any Man Because I Have Been To The Mountain Top." I remember telling Kay I believe I saw death on his face. She didn't believe me, but Reverend King was assassinated the next day. On the second day after King's death, riots broke out all over the country. We had some problems in Michigan, but it was nothing compared to the Detroit riot of 1967. After the death of Reverend King, Black folks became very militant, they were angry because they knew that the FBI was out to destroy Reverend King, just as some of us believe they had had Malcolm X killed. I think it was sometime in 1969, when the FBI and some police officers murdered Fred Hampton and Mark Clark in their sleep. It seemed as if all the country's law enforcement officers had declared war on Black Americans.

I KNEW MY FATHER WAS DYING

In 1970, I received a phone call from my father. He wanted me to meet him in Indianapolis so that we could visit my oldest brother in prison. This was a strange request; My brother had been incarcerated in prisons all across the country and this was the first time my father had wanted to visit him. I remember on several occasions, when my grandmother wanted my father to go and see about my brother. He always refused to go. I remember him saying, "Junior is a grown man, and I have to take care of my other children." I can't describe how much my grandmother loved my brother. I remember she once went behind my father's back and paid a white lawyer to try and get my brother out of jail in Pennsylvania. My father found out what she had done, and tried to get her money back. I remember going to the lawyer's office with my father. I believe he gave the money back to my father. When I saw my father, I knew why he wanted to see my brother. My father was dying.

My brother was in prison for killing a white man. I never knew the details of what happened. One of my brothers who also lived in Indianapolis said, my brother shot a white man who died a year later, and my brother was sentenced to seven to fifteen years in prison. My father, mother, two brothers, and I drove to Michigan State Prison. My brother was surprised and glad to see us. When we left for the drive back to Indianapolis, my father said something that I didn't understand at the time. He said to my mother, "Junior has not changed." I now realize my father was talking about my brother's gay lifestyle.

I knew I was losing my father and I didn't have any photos of him and I wanted something by which to remember him. In December of 1970, I brought a camera and went home. I took a lot of pictures of my father and other family members. I really enjoyed my time with him. That was the last time I saw him alive. I also tried to get my brothers to realize we were losing our father, but they were in denial and didn't believe me. My father's health was gradually deteriorating. He smoked two packs of camel cigarettes per day, and hard work and alcohol had taken a toll on his health. He also suffered from emphysema and a heart condition. Sometime he would have such bad coughing spells, I thought he would pass out.

Even during his illness my father still tried to maintain his dignity. He was a very proud man. When I went home he was always glad to see me. My father always made me feel good, because I knew he loved me. Some of my brothers used to tell me I was my father's favorite child. I never believed that he favored me, my father just knew he could depend on me. He didn't have much faith in my brothers. He knew I would always be there for him. There have been times in my life when I believed that my brothers hated me, even today I am not close to any of them.

THE JEALOUSY OF MY BROTHERS

I have always felt threatened by my brothers because they would often attack me physically when we had a disagreement. When I was a child they often struck me, even after I became an adult they would still threaten me. Even today I don't like being around them. After I left Alabama and returned to Detroit, my mother called me about twice a week. She was worried about my father's health. She could see that he was getting weaker every day and he wasn't eating. My father was always very thin. When I was a child I don't remember him eating very much. It seemed that we never had enough food. My father would take food off his plate and divide it amongst the children. I often heard him tell my mother to give his food to us because he wasn't hungry. I am sure my father went to work hungry many days.

When I look back on his life I can feel his pain and how he must have suffered. During this period the conditions for the Black man in the South were so bad that it was beyond my comprehension. The effect of the Jim Crow laws was something no human being should have experienced. I don't believe Black Americans today have any idea how much our people have suffered. I never heard my father complain about his condition; he just worked harder to try and make life better for his family.

I think it was in 1970 when President Nixon closed all

the OEO offices. Some of my co-workers found other jobs, but most of us were grand fathered into the Department of Social Services as clerks. I worked as a receptionist at the front desk. After I took the Civil Services test, I was hired as an eligibility worker (ADC caseworker). I think I had been with the agency for about a year when my brother called to let me know that my father had suffered a heart attack. I was getting ready to go home and was scheduled to leave the next day, when I got a phone call from my mother. She said that she had just left the hospital, and the last thing my father said to her was, "Don't forget to phone Loraine and tell her not to come down here because I am going to be all right." I could not leave right away because I could not get plane reservations. I was planning to leave the next day. My father passed away that same night, December 4, 1971.

THE DEATH OF MY FATHER & THE ATTICA UPRISING—PRISON RIOT

There are two things that stand out in my mind in the year of 1971—my father's death and the Attica uprising. The rebellion started on September 11, 1971, and lasted for five days. I believe it was the worse prison riot that ever happened in this country. I will discuss it later when I talk about my relationship with Shango, one of the Attica brothers. When I arrived home for the burial of my father, my family was in chaos. My brothers were drinking and trying to give my mother advice, and she wouldn't listen to anyone. My mother always had to have things her way. When my father was alive he always supported her. It didn't matter if she was right or wrong. When I realized what my mother was trying to do, I had to agree with my brothers. My mother wanted to take my father's body back to Athens, Alabama. Our family had been living in Anniston for about thirty years; all my father's friends lived in Anniston. Most of the people my father knew who lived in Decatur-Athens were either dead or their whereabouts unknown.

My mother was determined to have his funeral in the church where they got married. Several carloads of his friends and family drove to Athens. A few older people from Decatur-Athens attended the services. Most of the people were friends and family from Anniston. My father was buried in the graveyard next to the church. There was so much turmoil in my family that I just wanted to bury my father and go home.

Several months later when my mother and brothers went to Athens to clean his grave and put a tombstone on it, the church was gone and they were running a highway though the land where the church had been. We will never know what happen to the body of my father. I think my mother regretted taking my father's body to Decatur-Athens. When my brother died, my mother bought a family cemetery plot in Anniston. When my mother passed away, we buried her there. My oldest brother and my sister did not attend my father's funeral. We couldn't find my brother. He had been released from prison the previous year and my sister was living in Washington D. C. My sister and her husband were drinking heavily. I wired her money for a plane ticket, but she didn't show up. I was very angry with her and said some very hateful things to her. When I returned home I was a nervous wreck.

My father came to me in a vision or a dream (everybody tells me it had to be a dream, but I don't remember being asleep). My father said to me, "Loraine I want you to remember, I love all my children the same, I want you to forgive your sister." I wrote my sister a long letter and asked her to forgive me for the things I said to her. I also realize now that I had an obnoxious attitude and that I played a large part in creating the attitude that my family had towards me (my self-righteousness attitude). I had a lot of problems with my whole family. I also understand now that the dysfunctional behavior in the black family is due to the legacy of slavery and Jim Crow. It will take many years and great determination for black families to overcome the effect of slavery.

It is sad to see Black Americans exhibiting such hatred toward each other. In most cases they don't have any understanding of what's happening to them. Self-hatred has done a lot of damage to my people. On occasions I have felt this hatred from my friends and family members. It really scares me. I think I need to give some information about my relationship with my sister. My mother was deeply hurt from the lost of my father and she had to take care of my sister's two teenage children. They were my sister's oldest children. My sister finished high school in 1955 and spent two years at A & M College in Huntsville, Alabama. She dropped out of college, went home pregnant, and had a baby boy. When she left home she was pregnant again. She left her baby boy with my parents and went to Detroit. A few months later gave birth to a girl. I think this was in 1957 or 1958. I was not in Detroit at this time because Robert and I had moved to Kentucky. I think her baby was about six or eight months old when my family got a phone call from a family friend who was also living in Detroit. They told my parents my sister was neglecting her baby and that she sometimes left the baby in the apartment alone. My father sent my mother to Detroit to get the baby and both children remained with my parents from that time on. My sister's oldest child, Bill, was about thirteen or fourteen years old when my father died, and Geraldine was about eleven or twelve.

My parents spoiled both children. I now believe that my parents were too old for the task of trying to raise two teenagers. After my parents took the children, my sister moved to Virginia, where she met her husband. After marriage, they moved to Washington, D.C. and my sister began the process of trying to take her children away from my parents, but they refused to let her have them. My sister and her husband had two children (boys), and my sister and her husband were running the streets (having a so-called good time). My sister said that her husband's family helped them with the boys when they lived in Virginia. My sister and her husband eventually became alcoholics (both of them are dead). My sister often told me she was sorry about neglecting her children. I noticed the difference in the behavior of the children raised by my parents, and the two children raised by my sister and her husband. The two children, raised by my sister and her husband, were very independent, and the children raised by my parents clung to my mother, especially the boy. The girl eventually got married, but the boy lived with my mother until she died.

THE ATTICA REBELLION
AND SHANGO'S TRIAL

When I first became involved in the civil rights movement, I thought I was helping to make some real changes in this country. I truly believed America could change. I am now seventy-two years old and have concluded that white supremacy and racism is deeply rooted in the fabric of this country. Not only in the hearts and minds of White Americans, but also in the courts, schools, government and private institutions.

I think I met Jim Ingram sometime in 1972 or 1973. It was after the Attica uprising. He had a radio show on a White station, and they were trying to take his show off the air. It was called "Drumbeat," and his commentary was always on Black issues. He also wrote for the Michigan Chronicle, a Black owned newspaper. A friend of mine introduced me to Jim. She was trying to help keep Jim's show on the air. Jim had become very popular in the Black community. She asked me to help get signatures on a petition to help keep his show on the air. Because I liked what he was saying, I worked hard and was able to get a lot of people to sign the petition.

Jim was also involved with the Attica brothers. The Attica rebellion started on September 11, 1971 and lasted for five days. Approximately one thousand prisoners seized the prison in an attempt to make demands for better living conditions. Governor Rockefeller sent in the National Guard and state police. They went in and shot the prisoners down like they were dogs. I think about forty prisoners were killed along with several guards who had been held as hostages. That case has lingered in the courts for years. On January 4th, 2000, the state of New York agreed to pay the prisoners and their families eight million dollars for the injustice they suffered at the hands of the officials of the state of New York. Almost one hundred prisoners and several guards suffered injuries, and there were also about sixty indictments against the prisoners, most of the charges were for murder and kidnapping.

Jim had risen to celebrity status in Detroit. During the Attica rebellion some of the Attica brothers asked Jim to come to the prison to hear their side of the story, because the White owned newspapers were anti-prisoners and were blaming the prisoners for everything. He couldn't go. Jim was very angry and militant. In 1967 he got caught up in the Detroit riot and took a horrible beating at the hands of several White policemen. Jim recovered from that beating and passed away about three or four years ago. He was in his late forties or early fifties. He was a very good friend and I still miss him.

Jim introduced me to Reverend Mother Smith; she was the mother of one of the Attica brothers. Mother Smith and I became good friends. She had a small church and a charity mission located on Linwood Avenue in the heart of the ghetto. Mother Smith still operates the charity mission and we keep in contact with each other. She feeds the homeless and gives clothes to any needy person in the community. This sister is a true humanitarian. Her son was the first prisoner to go on trial in New York for the Attica uprising. Mother Smith asked me to go to New York with her to attend his trial. During that time I met her son Bernard Strobe (a.k.a. Shango Bahati Kakawana), he was still in prison in New York for his action in Courtyard-D. Shango was charged with four counts of murder and one count of kidnapping.

On September 23, 2001, Showtime made a movie (Killing Yard), about Shango's action in Courtyard-D and in the New York courtroom. I was happy that Showtime decided to do a movie on Shango, but they could never show the real essence of the Shango I knew. He was also shot in Courtyard-D. I thank God for the privilege of having this brother in my life. I was closer to Shango than I was to my blood brothers. Shango took his name from the Santeria religion, which is practiced in Cuba, and was brought from Africa by the slaves. Shango is the warrior god, which came from the Yoruba culture in Nigeria. Shango is the god who rules lightning, thunder, and virility. At Shango's trial, Earnest Goodman, a member of a law firm located in Detroit, represented Shango. I had never attended a trial of this magnitude; news reporters took up most of the seats in the courtroom, and policemen with dogs surrounded the courthouse. Prior to entering the courtroom, each person was required to submit to a bodily search.

Shango participated in his own defense; on several occasions the judge gave him permission to question some of the jurors. Shango conducted himself with the utmost dignity and intelligence. He made me feel proud to be a Black woman. The jury was made up of ten Whites and two Blacks. Shango was acquitted of all charges. All members of the jury attended the victory party. Shango could not attend the party because he was waiting for them to return him to Detroit, where he was charged with shooting two White policemen. I think one of the policemen is still alive today.

Shango was extradited from New York to stand trial in Detroit. There is a statute that says a prisoner's trial must be held within one hundred and twenty days of his arrival in the receiving state. If the trial cannot be held within one hundred and twenty days, the prosecutor must request a continuance and show good cause in open court as to why a continuance beyond the one hundred days should be granted. Shango's trial was not held within the one hundred days as required by law; nor was there any continuance requested or granted.

For that reason, Shango's attorney motioned for a dismissal; a recorder's court judge denied the motion, without rendering an opinion as to why. The issue was then taken to both the Michigan Court of Appeals and Michigan Supreme Court, and they both affirmed Shango's conviction without granting a hearing or allowing arguments to be heard on the issue. On February 17, 1978 Shango's lawyers appealed to the Sixth Circuit Court of Appeals in Cincinnati, Ohio. Again the best lawyers in the country, Professor Haywood Burns and former U.S. Attorney General Ramsey Clark, represented him. I attended the hearing in Cincinnati. The Court of Appeals in Ohio overturned his murder conviction and he was freed in 1979.

Shango's freedom meant a lot to me. This happened at a time when I had just been fired from the Department of Social Services and had a lot of time on hand. Shango and I spent a lot of time together. We talked about everything, and he taught me a lot about the prison system. I don't believe the average person, Black or White, really understands the full impact this system has on the life of an individual. Presently, they are building more prisons than schools. The primary purpose of prison is to use inmates for slave labor; most of the state prisons are being run by private businesses. There are currently about two million people in prison in this country, and most of them are Black or other minorities.

Shango became involved with some brothers from the Black National Movement, and I attended some of the meetings with him. Whenever Minister Farrakhan was in town, we went to hear him speak. We heard him speak several times at King Solomon Baptist Church. I was unemployed at this time and spent most of my spare time with Shango. Sometimes he came over to my apartment and we talked all night long. I want to make it clear that Shango and I were never involved in a romantic relationship. I think that is why our friendship was so special, and I learned so much from him. During this time I was also dealing with the case involving my firing from the Department of Social Services. I can very truthfully say that during my grievance hearings there were only two individuals who attended all the hearings: Edward Vaughn and Shango.

I realized that a lot of people could not attend because of the distance; the grievance hearings for state employees were held in Lansing, Michigan. It was also during this period that I was in the process of trying to move to Africa. I was going to and from Africa on a regular basis. I think I had a hearing sometime in 1979. I had just recently returned to this country for a hearing; it was during this period when Shango told me he was going to be killed. He would often say, "If a Black man kills a police officer in this country he will never be free, or he will never walk the streets again." Shango's mother and I started calling him paranoiac; but that didn't stop him from saying he was going to be killed.

I think it was sometime in 1981 that I broke my ankle in Africa. I went to the hospital and they set my leg in Africa, but it wasn't healing properly, and I had to return to this country for medical care. I had given up my apartment in Detroit and had to go to my mother's house to wait for my ankle to heal. One night in December I had a dream about Shango. I dreamed Shango's mother and I were looking for him. We found him in a house on West Grand Blvd. When he saw us he smiled and said: "Ameenah I don't want you and mother worrying about me, because I am going to be o.k." The following day I received a phone call from Edward Vaughn informing me about Shango's death; Shango had been killed on December 1,1982, from a shotgun blast to the back of his head. After his death, the Detroit newspapers tried to demonize him. One paper called him, "A one man crime wave, and the meanest man that ever moved through Detroit Recorder Court." The authorities always found ways to make Black men look and act like demons, because they have no idea what it's like to live the life of a Black man in America. The condition the Black man is subjected to is enough to make him mean and angry.

I understand very well how Shango felt. If he was a killer, they made him a killer. If I had been born a Black male, I probably would have been a killer or they would have destroyed me a long time ago. The Detroit Free Press said that Shango was killed while trying to get drug dealers out of his mother's building, but I will always believe that Shango's death had nothing to do with drug dealers; he was assassinated by the Detroit Police Department or they put a contract out on him. Shango's death affected me deeply, I still miss him, and he will always be a dear friend. I am going to include a speech Shango gave me on the third anniversary of the Attica rebellion, Shango was still in jail, but this speech was read by Jim Ingram at a memorial service on September 13, 1974 in Buffalo, N.Y.: *"Oh! How courageous were you my brothers, the world outside will never truly know. No! They will never truly know! They will never know the gallantry you displayed, even with the imminence of death menacingly beaming down upon you, yet not one detection of fear accompanied your rain coated face. In itself, that was a remarkable achievement of incomparable strength and fortitude. Yes, you scintillate most brilliantly my brothers in our hearts this 13th day of September 1974: the anniversary of your memorial day. And for you we have vowed in your name, not to let one mind rest or feel diminished until we have carried out your will, and have given reality to your thoughts, objectives and aims. No! The world outside will never truly know. They will never truly know and understand the entertainment of your mind and the pre-occupation of your hearts. Why? Simply because they are not made of the same fabric as yourself; A fabric which enabled you to conceive and understand the destructive magnitude of oppression, racism and repression, and to tender a spirit and will to fight against it, without fear or an individualistic motivation of self interest. A fabric woven out of threads of incredible hardship and perpetual suffering manufactured and produced by the nefarious tentacles of capitalism-political, racial, and dominion. No! They couldn't know the elements which impelled that act of rebellion since they have not experienced the daily antagonism you were forced to endure or tasted the bitterness of its reality. All of their cries and thunderous outrage are merely sentiments based on the factuality of your humanity. Their conscious intellect tells them of your humanize, however, unfailingly a note of peculiarity of incomplete comprehension seems to emerge from that bit of consciousness. This fact recoils me in sadness. No! They will never truly know in so much as their hearts do not function with the same capacity for life as did yours, my brothers, what has made you/us strong has damn near destroyed their very nature? And in their callousness and insensitivity, they have become a creation of an unnatural sort. Moreover, they were not there to witness the fact, what actually occurred; how you stood bravely in the face of perhaps the greatest single atrocity in history. An unmerciful slaughter, barbaric in character and savage in nature, perpetrated on unarmed men who found themselves in a totally inoffensive position. We think of their lives and action as dramatizing and summarizing the spirit and likeness of: Lumumba, Malcolm X, George and Jonathan, Nancy Ling Perry, Clinque, Twymon Myers, Nat Turner, Bobby Hutton, John Brown, and so many other lives which have been motivated by a deep human love and an unquenchable thirst for freedom, not just for self, but a world freedom for all. Yes, they have exemplified courage in a most grandiose revolutionary style. And yes, they are the nucleus of our thought process— and we shall proceed forever in the wake of their memory, armed in spirit and prepared in struggle."*

On December 3, 2000, the state of New York paid eight million dollars to the Attica brothers and their surviving relatives. More than a quarter of a century after the deadly Attica prison riots. Thirty prisoners and 11 prison employees were killed, all shot by state police. Some of the employees and prisoners were brutally beaten by the police.

MY THOUGHTS ON RELIGION, MEN AND RACISM

When I celebrated my seventieth birthday, I had been writing for two years, trying to tell my life story. At first I thought it would be an easy task; I soon discovered it was a very difficult and trying undertaking. There has been a time when it has been very painful, especially when I try to write about brothers and sisters who are no longer in their physical form (dead). However, I strongly believe that their spirits are very much alive. I am going to use an expression from my father, he often said, "we are spirits wrapped in human flesh." I did not understand what he meant when he used that expression. However, the meaning becomes clearer as I grow older and become more in tune to my own spirituality.

Most of the time when I attempt to discuss spirituality with most Black people, they seem to think I am talking about a ghost or something supernatural, or they think I'm talking about the so-called "Holy Ghost," as it is taught in the Christian Church. I am not a Christian. Once upon a time I studied the Islamic faith. I still believe the Islamic faith is one of the purest religions in the world. But in recent years I made up my mind not to worship any god in which the religious teaching gives men the right to exploit women. I cannot believe in just a male god. I believe it is a combination of a superior force that's both male and female.

The world has been dominated and controlled by men because of their physical strength and world domination; I also believe women have given men power to rule over them because they thought it was the way things were meant to be. When I first went to Africa I wanted to see how Islam was taught and practiced there. I experienced a lot of problems because I was traveling alone. Almost everything is controlled and run by men, and it is even worse in the Middle East. Most women have a hard time just trying to survive without the help of a man. When I first visited some of the villages in Africa, I noticed many young girls were married to old men. In some cases their families gave the girls to these old men.

I think it was in 1974 or 1975 when I became more aware of the Department of Social Services' racist policies. We had two unions in the agency (WEU) Welfare Employee Union, and (AFSCME) Michigan State Employees Association, I became a member of AFSCME because it was a national union and they represented federal and state employees all across the country. The employee union representatives were two White militants. The one I worked with most of the time was Tom, and he convinced me to become a union representative. Whenever an employee had a problem with the supervisor, we would try to resolve the problem without filing a grievance; if it involved all the employees, we would hold a meeting with all the employees. For example: when we didn't have any heat in the building, we organized all the employees and everyone walked out of the building with us. At that time I think there were approximately two hundred people employed in that district; it was the largest district on the east side of Detroit.

I also worked with a sister who was a union steward for WEU. It was also during this period that I became more aware of "institutional racism," and how it was practiced against both the Black employees and our clients. In order for them to get away with their racist policies, they would place Blacks in positions of authority; the same behavior was practiced during slavery, when Blacks were placed in positions of authority for the sole purpose of controlling the slaves. The same thing is happening today in federal and state institutions, and Black folks are winning law suits all across the country because of institutional racism in the work place.

I was always classified as a good worker; I received good and outstanding ratings every six months. I had been with the agency for seven years and never received a promotion. The first six years I worked under White supervision. The last White supervisor gave me nine outstanding ratings in all categories, and that was rare for any worker, but management was determined to fire me. They did everything they could to make my supervisor fire me, but she refused. Ms. Simpson always said I was one of her best workers. During the last two years with the agency I had all kinds of problems with management, but never with my immediate supervisor. They finally placed me under a black supervisor, Ms. Terry, for the sole purpose of firing me.

I was fired from the Department of Social Services sometimes in 1978. I am not sure of the month and day because I was dealing with a lot of emotional stress. I was very angry because my co-workers did not support me. The only support I received was from a few Whites and the Black sisters from the Welfare Employee Union. I realize now most of my co-workers didn't support me because they were afraid of losing their jobs. Edward Vaughan and Shango were the only friends who came to the hearings. Tom Suber represented me. Before the hearings were finally over, I really felt sorry for Ms.

Terry? The agency used her to get me, and Tom Suber made her look like a fool. When he questioned her, she became very angry and frustrated, and said: "I had to do what my boss told me to do," she often called her supervisor "boss."

When Mr. Seano realized they were losing the case, he told her in front of everybody, "I don't see how they ever made you a supervisor." That expression from that white man to this sister almost made me sick. He was representing the agency. I really learned some valuable lessons from that experience; I discovered that the friends and relatives of most Black folks have a tendency to believe that you created the problems when you are fired form a job. Some Black folks will take almost anything just for the sake of having a so-called good job. I can somewhat understand their attitude because most Black folks have to struggle to get a job, and they also have to struggle to keep the job.

It has been more than twenty years since I was fired from that agency, and there have been changes in some government and state jobs, but never enough, because the white racists will always be with us, as well as some Black folks who still believe in the superiority of the White race. It will be a long time before this behavior is eradicated from the minds of Black folks. It was also during this period that I began experiencing medical problems. I was dealing with lots of emotional stress, and my feet began to swell. I went to the doctor and discovered I had high blood pressure. It was also during this time in 1976 when I decided to have my name changed.

On May 24, 1977 my name was legally changed before the Honorable Frank S. Szymanski, Judge of Probate Court in the State of Michigan. I was determined to change my name before making my second trip to Africa; when I asked the agency to change my name on my employment records, all hell broke out. I think it took about a year before my name was changed on my personnel records. It was also during this period, that I felt the need to leave this country. I felt like I was slowly drinking poison. I knew America was destroying me. I was at the point where anger, despair and frustration were driving me to drink, and it frightened me because I knew alcoholism ran in my family.

In an attempt to get my drinking under control, I turned to religion. As far as I was concerned Christianity was out of the question. I began looking at Islam. I knew I needed help because the problem seemed to be bigger than me. I made a decision not to become involved in organized religion. When I went to West Africa, I noticed that people in most of the countries I visited practiced Islam, and they didn't appear to be caught up in the rhetoric of religion. For them, it was just a way of life. Everything in their life revolved around the teachings of Islam. I believe Islam is one of the purest religions in the world. But, in recent years I have rejected all religious faiths because all the books are written and interpreted by man. In my opinion this has kept most women under the worse kind of oppression.

I recently realized that I have had some very serious problems with males, and that has created serious problems for me in Africa and in some Middle Eastern countries. And it all started with Black men in this country. I have never been able to understand how they can abuse Black women. The Black woman has always been the only person who totally supported the Black man. When I look back over my life, I realize I have accepted a lot of abuse from Black men. I don't mean just physical abuse. To live in America the average female, Black or White, has to tolerate physical and emotional abuse from Black and White men. Since I have retired I refuse to accept any kind of abuse from any man. On my last job I had to accept a lot of emotional abuse—the director of the organization was a man. I will go into more details about the organization when I write about the last ten years of my work experience.

I believe a lot of men believe they have a god-given right to control women. I believe they exhibit this obnoxious behavior because of their physical strength. I also believe women themselves have given them a lot of power. I don't believe they deserve this power. We have wars, nuclear weapons, and pollution because of the White men; and that is only a small part of the damage he has done to the world. That's why I have difficulties accepting God in the image of a male. Some of the most insidious deeds that have happened in the world, happened because of the domination of the White male. Some of my friends and relatives tell me they believe I hate White people. To be honest, I don't see anything wrong with love or hate. I hate injustice, racism, and violence. I don't hate all White folks, because there have been some White individuals I really cared about. I love Kay like a sister. And it often pains me when I think of her, because I don't know if she is living or dead.

Whenever I hear White folks bragging about the so-called founding fathers, it makes me sick, because most of them owned slaves. Even today I still have problems understanding what kind of people would enslave and dehumanized another race of people just because of their skin color. It has to be a degenerate race of people. This leads me to believe that something happened that damaged the White man's spirit as a human being during the European biological evolution.

INCIDENTS THAT HAVE AFFECTED ME PERSONALLY AND 9/11 BEING ONE OF THEM

Today's date is March 26, 2002, about seven months since the 9/11 incident. My purpose for referring this event is because of how it has affected me personally.

Since the 9/11 incident, I have been dealing with a lot of emotional stress; this is the first time this kind of tragedy has ever happened on American soil, and I knew that the American government would take revenge by bombing some poor country. President Bush and his right wing bandits dropped tons of bombs on Afghanistan, a poor country that had recently come out of a war with Russia. The entire infrastructure had already been destroyed by that war, and the saddest part was the propaganda from the news media only made matters worse. The average American had no understanding of the type of devastation and destruction our country has caused in poor countries.

I went into the hospital on March 3, 2001; I had a virus or a cold. This was the third time I had been hospitalized since 1999. Because I have emphysema (forty years of smoking), I am on oxygen from eighteen to twenty four hours per day. Therefore, I am usually hospitalized whenever I have a virus or cold. I believe that is why I feel the urgency to complete *My Life Story;* one day I may go into the hospital for the last time. I feel it is necessary for me to write and express my feelings about any issue that has had an affect on me personally.

The AIDS epidemic is another issue that has really bothered me. I first heard about the AIDS virus in the earlier eighties. I had just returned to this country from Africa. I read everything I could find about the disease. I went to New York to visit a friend who was dying of AIDS, he was White and gay. I met him in the sixties. He was a member of the Worker World Social Party. After I returned to this country, we did some work together in Detroit. I called him and he asked me to come to New York to see him. I discovered that he had done extensive research on the disease. After talking with him and some of his friends, I believe that the AIDS virus is a man made disease. However, in later years I became convinced that some people in our government perpetuated genocide against the dark people of the world when they created this disease.

The devastation from the AIDS virus has had its toll in Africa. About thirty million people in Africa, South of the Sahara, are HIV positive. About one hundred and forty million people have already died from the AIDS virus in Africa. Another ten million are expected to die within the next five years. In Botswana, nearly twenty-five percent of the people are infected. In some parts of Africa, five to one thousand people are being buried every day. In Zimbabwe almost thirty percent of the people are infected with the AIDS virus. Although women represent about forty-five percent of the continent's population, they account for fifty-five percent of all AIDS cases.

Teenage girls have been hit hard by AIDS because older men prey upon them. They suffer five to six times more than men or boys. More than twelve million children under the ages of twelve have lost their mothers because of the AIDS virus. What's really sad is the fact that Africa does not have the resource to combat the epidemic.

It has become increasingly difficult for me to read anything about AIDS in Africa because of the pain I feel for the people in Africa. The devastation from this disease is beyond anything I have heard of in my lifetime, and this is all happening because of the sick mind of the White man. After I decided to move to Africa, I was still very angry. The years 1978 and 1979 were difficult years for me, spending most of my time in Africa, but I had to return to this country for my grievance hearings. I felt that most of my friends had turned their backs on me. I began to look towards Africa for love and friendship; I found both in Africa. I am not trying to romanticize Africa, because I had both good and bad experiences in Africa.

MY VISITS TO AFRICA

I have read a lot of books about Africa, and I still believe we can learn a lot from reading, but spending time in other countries' gave me a different perspective. Africa is not only a beautiful continent, but it seems ageless and appears to have existed forever. When the planet was created, it must have begun in Africa. I felt as if I had been away from home a long time. And I had finally come home. When I first saw the beautiful faces of the people; I realized this wasn't the first time I had seem them. They were people I had been dreaming about all my life. I first visited Dakar Senegal, West Africa in the early seventies. During that period there were very few Senegalese who could speak or understand English. On the first day of my arrival, I checked into the hotel and tried to order some food. They could not take my order because I could not speak French, and they could not speak English.

They finally sent someone to my room that could speak English. That is how I met Eloge. I told him this was my first visit to Africa, and he promised to give me a tour of the city; we became good friends. Eloge introduced me to his mother, his sister, and their families. He also introduced me to a couple of young sisters whose grandmother lived on Goree Island. They introduced me to their grandmother; she was almost a hundred years old (Goree Island is located across from Dakar,

Senegal, the place Africans were held before they were put on the slave ships to cross the Atlantic to America). Their grandmother was called "the grandmother of the island." When we visited her, she invited me into her home. She showed me photos of some dead relatives, and she also showed me an old issue of Ebony that contained a story on her and Goree Island from the early sixties. Josephine, one of her granddaughters, said that her grandmother didn't usually invite strangers into her home. She also said her grandmother told her that she invited me into her home because I had a pure spirit. I didn't understand what she meant by that statement and I often wonder today about that remark. But I can remember that event as if it happened today.

I also traveled to several other countries in West Africa (Gambia, Ghana, Sierra Leone, Nigeria, Liberia, and Togo). I have spent as long as six to nine months in some countries. I also visited a couple of countries in East Africa, and several countries in North Africa (Libya, Egypt, and Israel). I traveled to all West African countries alone. I think that is why I experienced so many problems with men in West Africa. There were some situations where I was asked the whereabouts of my husband. When I told them that I didn't have a husband and that I was traveling alone, they seemed to be surprised. I traveled to Egypt with Tony Bruder's group, and to Libya with a Muslim group. In most African and Middle Eastern countries women are completely controlled by men. And, at that time they couldn't do anything without the consent of their husbands or fathers. In most of the countries I met some wonderful people.

I love Senegal and Ghana because of the friendships I was able to establish there. I had some very interesting experiences in Africa. When I look back at that time some of the incidents were very funny, but at the time it happened it really scared me. When I first went to Africa, I went with the same arrogant attitude that is exhibited by both Black and White Americans; we exhibit this negative behavior in our body language and gestures. I don't believe we are aware of this behavior until we have spent time in the cultural environment of other countries. I thank my Creator for Eloge and other friends who cared enough about me to take the time to teach me. When I look back at that time, I realize the result of my obnoxious behavior created all kind of problems for me.

One incident I will never forget happened to me on my first trip to Africa. Eloge had warned me not to take my camera out unless I was with him. One morning I went out walking alone, the people were so beautiful, I decided to take some pictures. I was standing in front of a super market waiting for it to open when I noticed two beautiful men standing across the street. I snapped their picture. They looked up and appeared to be very angry. They came across the street and took my camera and took me to jail. This was my worse nightmare and I could not even communicate with them. The people at the jail finally helped me understand that I did not have permission to take their picture. They took my camera and allowed me to leave; I didn't stop running until I got back to the hotel. That evening Eloge went to the police station to find out what happened. He tried to get me to go with him, but I was too scared. They explained to him what had happened and gave him my camera. I think this is why I don't have many pictures of Africa. There have been times when I didn't take any pictures at all.

Most of the time whenever I talk about Africa, there is always someone to remind me of the terrible conditions in Africa: famine, poverty, and wars. I believe Africa will eventually move in a more positive direction when they stop allowing themselves to be exploited by Europeans. The Europeans are the same people who took the native people out of Africa and reduced them to slavery, and colonized and carved up the whole continent of Africa. During the Berlin Conference of

1884, the Continent of Africa was divided up among the European nations for the sole purpose of taking control of Africa's resources.

During that time Britain, France, German, Portugal and Belgium totally dominated Africa. They took out the gold, diamonds and artifacts that made the European countries rich. At that time Africa was too weak to defend herself. The Europeans killed million of Africans because they didn't have firearms to defend themselves. And we also have to remember that the colonization of Africa lasted for over a hundred years.

I remember when Ghana gained her independence. I think it was in 1957, I can't remember the month, but I felt very proud of Ghana. I read in the newspaper about Dr. Ralph Bunch going to Ghana for the celebration, I think Dr. Bunch was the American representative to the United Nations. Most of the other Africa countries gained their independence in the early sixties. I am still amazed that we are in the new millennium and we still have some Black Americans who still think that Africa is just as it has been portrayed in the Tarzan movies. Sometimes we exhibit this kind of negative behavior because of the negative images we see on American television.

I SPENT 22 YEARS TRAVELING
TO AND FROM AFRICA

I am having problems writing about my experience in Africa. I spent about twenty-two years traveling to and from Africa, however, I am not able to write each incident in chronological order because so many things happened, for which I can remember the incident but not the date or the year. I realize now that I should have kept a journal. When I went to Egypt I can remember almost everything that happened because I was only there for a short period of time.

There is one other experience that I will never forget; I was in Ghana in 1981 when they had the bloodless coup ever. I had a lot of Ghana's money, but it was worthless, there wasn't anything to buy, not even food. The people only had a little white rice and in most cases they didn't have cooking oil to cook the rice (most of the people used small oil stoves for cooking). I saw hunger all over the country. I was living at the Nkrumah Motel in Accra. It was an inexpensive motel. I think I lived there for about four or five months.

Most of the people from the previous government were trying to leave the country. I had to stay away from my friends because the police were coming to the motel to see me everyday. They were trying to get diamonds and wanted me to help them smuggle gold out of the country. They also wanted the names of my friends (most of my friends were scheduled to start working for the new government). The authorities from the old government were arresting some of them. When I refused their request, they got angry and wouldn't let me leave the country. When I arrived at the airport, on the day I was scheduled to leave, they would not allow me to board the plane. They locked me in a room. The only way I could communicate with my friends, and they with me, was by writing on a notebook and holding it up to the window.

My friends got in contact with a professor from the University of Ghana who arranged to help me get out of the country. The following night the professor and a friend drove me to Klouto, and from there I crossed the border into Togo, and finally made my way back to Senegal. I remember taking a bus in Klouto to get to Togo. It was early in the morning and they were selling beer on the bus. There was a big fire in a can sitting in the middle of the bus. I was real scared. I had never seen anything like this before.

There was another incident that I can remember so

well. I was going by bus to visit Eloge's Uncle, who lived in Benin. I was scheduled to change buses at the border. When we reached the border, I discovered that there was no place to sit, just a big field and a small shack where they stamped your passport and visa. When I gave them my passport to stamp, one of the male clerks asked me my nationality. I told him I was Afro-American, and he said to me, "You are not an African, you are just an American." I was tired from standing out in the sun and riding on the bus for four or five hours. I became angry and began using profanity. He refused to return my passport and continued to hold it until my bus was full. When I was finally able to get on the bus I had to sit on the back where they had live chickens hanging across their backs. When I arrived in Benin; my back was covered with chicken mess. When I told Eloge's uncle what happened, he was very angry. This is just an example of some of the incidents I experienced.

WHAT VISITING EGYPT DID FOR ME

Egypt and Libya were the most interesting countries I ever visited. My trip to Egypt reinforced my faith in the superior power of the Black people who inhabited that country. I was impressed with the ancient statues and monuments. I believe they were left for the purpose of allowing human kind to see the images and handwork of our Creator. And I don't have any doubt in my mind that they were Black people. My spiritual awareness was overwhelming. There has never been any time in my lifetime that I desired to be of another race, but, for the first time I was proud and glad to be of the Black race. I have never seen anything that made me feel what I felt in Egypt. All the statues looked like Black folks. The same Black folks who have always been a part of me all of my life. I saw some places that gave me cold chills. I took some beautiful photographs of Egypt. Most of my friends who have seen the photographs tell me that they are the best pictures I have ever taken.

Libya is another country that was interesting. After visiting Libya, I came back to this country with terrible images in my mind and a pain in my soul; this was in 1987, the year this country dropped tons of bombs on another small country. I traveled to Libya with a Muslim group and a few militant Blacks. Muammar Gadhafi was demonized by the news media in 1986, during the Reagan Administration. This was when this government, in an attempt to justify the bombing of Libya, used the bombing of a discotheque in Germany. At the time I visited Libya, Americans were forbidden to go to that country, but I went anyway because I really wanted to see a country that had been bombed. I don't think the American people have a clue how much damage a bomb causes; everything dies: children, animals, and the environment.

They bombed neighborhoods, hospitals, and they killed Gadhafi's nine-month-old baby. Thousands of innocent civilians were killed without mercy. When I visited Tripoli I saw hundreds of people laying in the streets waiting to be treated by doctors because the hospitals had been destroyed. I saw babies and children with arms and legs blown off. I remember on our way home some members of the group were concerned about being arrested for traveling to Libya. I was too angry to be scared. Every time I hear about this country bombing a poor country it almost makes me physically ill.

Sometimes I feel like two people. My spirit seems to take complete control over the way I think. There have been times when I went back and read what I had written, and could not remember having written it. At first it bothered me because I felt as if I were losing my mind; it doesn't bother me anymore, because it has been happening for years. However, I have concluded that some of us were born with an old spirit. I have had some experiences that I have never shared with anyone because I didn't want anyone calling me crazy, because I could not deal with that kind of abuse. I have also seen things and felt the presence of other spirits. Please understand that I am not talking about the so-called "ghost" of dead people, or the supernatural. I believe there is a spiritual reality that is only meant for me. I also believe in the spirits of our ancestors. I believe all of our great athletes and entertainers excel only because of the power and spirits of our ancestors. I have only discussed this with a very few people because some of our people have serious problems discussing anything that they don't understand.

About thirty years ago a friend of mine asked me to attend a lecture at the Detroit Museum to hear a representative from Self-Realization Fellowship. Paramahansa Yogananda founded the organization. I attended the lecture several times and bought his book entitled *The Autobiography of A -Yoga*. I read the book and was impressed with his writing. But, I soon forgot about it. However, in the last ten years I have read the book twice and several other books on "spirituality." While reading these books I discovered a lot of information that gave me greater insight into my own spirituality.

In 1987 I had a very strange experience; one Friday morning I went to work sick and by noon I was to sick too finish the day. I got permission to go home. I thought I was coming down with a cold. On my way home I stopped at the drug store and bought some over-the-counter cold medicine. When I got home I took the medication, left my radio playing, and went to bed. When I woke up I noticed gospel music was playing. I was still very sick and kept asking myself, why are they playing gospel music on Saturday morning. When I managed to get out of bed, I noticed water jars and ice trays all over my apartment and a washcloth and rubbing alcohol was on the table by my bed. I finally realized it was Sunday morning and wondered what had happened to Saturday? That is one day in my life that I can't remember.

I asked the manager of my building to help me get to the hospital. I went to the hospital and they put me in intensive care immediately, because they had to get my fever down. I later realized that Friday night and all day Saturday I was trying to get my fever down. Whenever I had a fever I would drink lots of cold water and use ice packs. If that didn't work I would give myself alcohol baths. At that time I didn't understand how I could have done those things without any remembrance of them. I realize now that my spirit was doing those things.

I ALMOST DIED

I made my last trip to Africa in 1998, I became very sick in Africa and remained sick the entire time I was there. I returned to this country October 10, 1998 and two days later I went into the hospital. I was diagnosed with pneumonia. I don't think I realized how sick I was until they transferred me to intensive care. I almost died. After they put me in my room, the nurse told me that he would be outside the door if I needed anything. I thought it was strange for him to spend the night outside my door. When I went to sleep I had a strange dream; I dreamt I was in this strange place and I saw a jazz band (I love jazz and gospel music). They seemed to be trying to tell me I had to find my way back home. When I woke up, I knew I was dying.

The next morning the doctor told me he had to double my medication because my white blood count was up to over seven thousand and I was still in the danger zone. I knew it wasn't time for me to leave this world; I had some things to do. At that time I didn't know the answer or what I had to do, I kept thinking that no one would really care if I lived or died. I only have three brothers living, we were not close, and I seldom heard from them. And most of my close friends are dead or still living in Detroit. I tried hard not to feel sorry for myself. Before I was released from the hospital they told me my lungs had been damaged by my years of smoking, and I had to be on oxygen from eighteen to twenty four hours a day. The doctor said the only thing that saved me was the fact that I had a strong heart and I needed the oxygen to save my heart. I was determined I wasn't going to let anyone put a handicap on me. When I arrived home, I called the oxygen company and asked them to remove the oxygen from my house.

About six months later I became ill again. My family doctor convinced me I had to use the oxygen. I have learned to live with this impediment. I also believe some of my sickness has been the result of anxiety. My purpose for trying to deal with my sickness is because I believe it helped me to get in touch with my spirituality. And everything that happened to me was the result of my struggle to exist as a human being in an environment where woman are treated like second class citizens, not to mention the fact that I am a Black woman. So the odds of my living to a ripe old age are very slim. My sister and her husband are a prime example of how trying to escape can lead to alcoholism and death at a very early age.

After I moved to DC, my sister and I became very close. She and her husband had recently bought a house. During the process of buying the house, her husband got sick. I noticed my sister started losing weight. I kept thinking it was because of her husband's illness and the stress of buying the house. One day I went to see her new house. When I was ready to leave, she walked me to the door. During this period I had recently stop smoking, and I begged my sister to stop smoking. She said she would try, but said she knew it would be hard because she was worried about her husband. A couple of months later, her son called to tell me that she was in the hospital. I went to see her and she said the doctors were running tests to determine what was wrong with her.

A few days later she was told she had liver cancer. My sister was in so much pain. I knew she was dying and went to see her everyday. I suffered right along with her. As soon as I walked into her room, she would ask me to rub her stomach. She said it made her feel better. About two days before her death, I got real sick. I didn't have any pain. But I became very weak and had a very high fever, and was suffering from flu-like symptoms. During that period I had a close friend living in this country from Damona Israel. She is a very spiritual individual. When she came over to see me and I described my symptoms to her, she said when I rubbed my sister stomach; I pulled negative energy into my body from the cancer. On the night she died, I was so sick I had to go to the emergency room. They gave me an examination and said they didn't understand what was causing the fever? They gave me an x-ray. I was too sick to stand up for the x-ray and had to take it lying down. They kept me overnight. The following morning when I went home, I got the news that my sister had died that night. I was still very ill and was too sick to attend her funeral.

Although the events associated with my illness were very painful, I am convinced that everything that happened in my life has been for a divine purpose, and the Creator has given me this life to evolve into a higher level of my spirituality.

WHEN I WAS AWAY FROM HOME

During all my years away from home, I did not have a habit of writing letters to my family. When I first left home, I had a telephone installed in my parent's home. This was for the purpose of having the opportunity to stay in close contact with my family. On several occasions the phone had been disconnected because my brothers made excessive long distance calls, but I always had the services restored. While in Africa, I was not able to call home as often as I desired. Phone calls to and from Africa were very expensive. One night while I was sound asleep, I heard my mother call my name. I jumped up in an attempt to answer her. It scared me because it sounded as if she was in the room with me. I soon forgot about the incident.

The following week I called home. Before I go any further I will have to go back to the seventies; my father died December 4, 1971. I think it was a few years later when I received a phone call from my mother. She was worried about my brother; she asked me to go to Indianapolis to see about him because he was drinking heavily and having domestic problems. When I arrived in Indianapolis, I went directly to his home. And I discovered that his wife had put him out. I also had another brother living in Indianapolis. I phoned his house and asked him to help me look for him. We spent hours looking for him. We finally found him living in an apartment without any heat or electricity. His living conditions were very poor and he was an alcoholic. When I called my mother and informed her of his living conditions, she told me to send him home. He went back to Alabama to live with my mother. He was no longer able to work and applied for his social security benefits. So, when I phoned my mother from Africa, she said I would have to come home and help her with my brother. I told my mother that the other family members living in Anniston could help her. I had another brother with adult children who could help her. I was determined not to come back to this country at that time.

When I left this country, I gave up my apartment and was in the process of trying to move to Africa for good. I told my mother I wasn't coming home. I felt that I had always been there for my family when they needed me in the past, but I was too far away to run home everytime there was a crisis in the family.

MY PLANS TO GO TO ZIMBABWE

In the meantime I had met a sister from Zimbabwe and we talked a lot about her country. She convinced me to go to her country to look for employment. She said while seeking a job I could live with her family, and the opportunity was better because the majority of the people in her country spoke English. She had already spoken to her family about me. I decided to go to Zimbabwe. I made plane reservations on Pan-Am and Eloge went to the airport with me. During that time there was some kind of construction going on at the airport. My plane was scheduled to leave about two or three o' clock in the morning. In order to board the plane I had to walk out on the airfield. I am not sure what happen, but I fell and broke my ankle. When I looked around for help, I realized that I was the only person on the field. I started hollering until someone finally heard me. Lucky for me, Eloge had not left the airport. They had to come out on the field to pick me up.

Eloge carried me to the hospital and they discovered I had a broken ankle. They put my leg in a cast and put me up at the hotel. A Pan Am representative came to see me the following day to inform me about my medical situation. They would take care of all my medical expenses because I was carrying their ticket. They also sent an African sister to deal with my clothing situation. The night I was scheduled to leave for Zimbabwe all my clothes were on the plane. This sister went out and bought me some clothes to last until my clothes were returned to Dakar. During my stay at the hotel, I was in constant pain. I knew something was wrong. I could hardly stand on my leg, even with crutches. I phoned the states and spoke to a friend who is a doctor and explained the situation to him. He said he didn't believe my leg was set correctly. I think I had been at the hotel for about a month when I told the Pan Am representative I didn't believe my leg was set correctly, she spoke to her people and they decided to send me back to the States.

I RETURNED TO THE
STATES WITH A BROKEN LEG

I arrived in New York and went to a medical center. They took x-rays and said they had to reset my leg. I also discovered I had a broken rib, but it was too late to do anything about it. They put my leg in another cast. I had to go some place for my leg to heal; I didn't have any other choice but to go home to Alabama. When I arrived at my mother's house, the first thing she said to me was, "I knew you were coming home, even if you are all broken up. Ha. Ha." When I walked into my mother's home, I felt like I had walked into hell. My brother was drunk and using all kinds of profanity towards my mother. The situation in my mother's home was very bad and I didn't know how to deal with it. It would have been useless to talk to my brother. I discovered a long time ago that it was a waste of time to try to talk to an alcoholic. In most cases they can become very abusive. My brother couldn't do any physical damage to anyone; he would just start name-calling and using profanity.

My brother's health was rapidly deteriorating. My mother, my middle brother (he and his family lived in Anniston), and I had a long discussion on how to resolve the problem. We all became very frustrated because we didn't know what to do. I made a decision to take him to the doctor. My mother's doctor was a young black doctor who had just arrived in town. Everyone was impressed with him. I went to his office and explained the situation to him. He asked me to bring my brother in to see him. I told my mother and brother about the doctor's appointment and they promised to go with me because I had difficulties getting around. My leg was still in a cast and I still had to use crutches.

The day I was scheduled to take him to the doctor, my mother and brother refused to go with me. My brother was very angry and said he wasn't going any place with me. I called a cab and when the cab arrived I stood over him and threatened to hit him with my crutches if he didn't get in the cab. He got in the cab and swore at me all the way to the doctor's office. The doctor examined him and prescribed some medication for him. From the day I took him to the doctor until he died he never took another drink. Before his death, he thanked me for everything and told me he was glad I came home. He was dying from throat and lung cancer. He also asked me to forgive him for the things he said to me.

My brother owned stock in the company he worked for when he lived in Indianapolis. When the company was sold, they notified my brother that he was entitled to the money from the sale of his stocks. My brother was very ill. He phoned me and asked me to meet him in Indianapolis. He went to get his money. He stayed with my other brother who still lived in Indianapolis. When I saw my brother I knew he was dying. He was always a very small person, but when I saw him I cried because he was skin and bones. The cancer had spread and he couldn't eat because he had throat cancer. My mother had to process his food because he couldn't swallow. We slept in my brother's den and talked all night. He talked about things that I couldn't believe he remembered. We talked about our childhood days, about the abuse he suffered from trying to exist as a Black man in this country, and the difficult times he had because he couldn't read and write. I cried for my brother and he thanked me for helping him in school and that was the last time I saw him alive.

After my leg healed, I left the south and returned to Detroit. I think I remained in the south for about six months or more. I also made a decision not to return to Africa to live because I felt my mother needed me here. I moved in with some friends and was in the process of looking for an apartment when I begin to notice the devastating condition of the city. That was in 1982 when the teenagers burned the houses in Detroit. Downtown Detroit was almost like a ghost town. Prior to leaving Detroit I had lived there for twenty-five years, and I had a deep love for the city. There wasn't any place to buy food and all the neighborhood stores were gone.

During this period my sister who lived in D.C. had made contact with me prior to my leaving for Africa. She and her husband had stopped drinking. They stopped drinking sometime in 1978 or 1979. She and her husband had been alcoholics for years. I only visited her twice in D. C. The first time I visited her I was very frustrated about their drinking and the environment was bad. Her living condition almost made me sick. They lived in the worse part of D. C. There was very little furniture in her home. My sister had two boys by her husband; I think they were ten and twelve years old. When I arrived in D.C. it was early in the morning and my sister was drunk. The boys were trying to get ready for school. The youngest child was trying to dry his clothes for school on the radiator. I almost got physically sick from seeing my sister's living condition. I had to rent a room in a hotel.

The following day my sister and her boys came to see me at the hotel. She didn't remember my coming to her house. I felt so sorry for her. I had already told my mother about my sister's situation and how I felt she was neglecting her children. The next year I asked my mother if I could bring my sister's boys to Alabama to spend the summer with her. I felt it would be good for the boys. My parents had bought their home in the early sixties. They lived in a subdivision that was located on the outskirts of Anniston. Most of the residents had built their homes and the environment was good. It was beautiful with a big back and front yard. The boys had never been to Alabama.

I went to D. C. and got the children and carried them to Alabama. The children had been in Anniston for about a month when I received a phone call from my mother telling me to come and take the children out of her house. I think the boys were about ten and eleven years old and my mother couldn't handle the boys because they had been raised in the slums of D. C. I phoned my sister and explained the situation to her and she asked me to send them home. I think that was in 1975. I went to Alabama and asked my brother if he would look after the boys, he lived about a block from my mother's house. I had to make arrangements to send them back to D.C.

I think it was sometime in 1977 when my sister and her husband stopped drinking. My sister made contact with me while I was in Africa to let me know that she and her husband had stopped drinking, and that they were trying to get their life together. While I was in the south waiting for my ankle to heal, my sister and I begin to build a good relationship. This was the first time in years that my sister and I could communicate like sisters. I think I left the south sometime in 1982; I went back to Detroit and stayed with friends. I was in the process of looking for an apartment when my sister asked me to visit her. I was very disappointed with Detroit, a city I had once loved. Somehow it didn't seem like the same place. So I went to visit my sister. I think it was at that point when I decided to leave Detroit and relocate to D.C.

I think I arrived in D.C. sometime in 1983. I am thankful to my Creator that I had the opportunity to spend some time with my sister. My sister was working and her husband was giving her as much support as possibly (he was legally blind). His blindness was a result of alcoholism. My sister and her husband were very close; their boys were teen-agers who still lived at home. Her youngest son was in his last year in high school and her oldest son had dropped out of school. My youngest brother was also living with them. My sister was living in the projects in a two-bedroom apartment. I slept on a cot in the living room. Our living situation was crowded, but that didn't bother me because my sister and I had a good relationship. For the first time in years, I enjoyed living with my sister. I had a better relationship with my sister than with anyone else in my family; I thank my Creator for giving me the opportunity to spend seven wonderful years with my sister. My brother was not working and kept creating problems for my sister. Finally, he asked me to give him the money to go home. I think I had been in D.C. about two or three months when I decided to look for work.

MY SISTER HELPED ME TO GET A JOB

My sister introduced me to one of her friends; she was a Muslim sister. We liked each other and had a good line of communication. I told her about my need to find employment and she told me about an organization where she was doing volunteer work. She and the director were friends and he was looking for a social worker. She took my resume to the director. The following day, the contract monitor phoned me for an interview. The director and the contract monitor interviewed me. I went to work for the organization on February 13, 1984. I knew I was going to be hired for the position when I walked through the door. I will always remember the red, black and green flag hanging in the front entrance lobby.

When I saw the flag (the Black American Liberation Flag), I knew I was at home. The organization is a twenty-four hour therapeutic program, based on an African centered concept. There were several reasons why I fell in love with the program. First, they had an all black staff. Second, it was an all black program. After my negative experience with the Department of Social Services, I wasn't ready to go back into a white controlled institution. Third, I didn't have to change my ideology. The African centered concept is a methodology in which the individuals are re-educated by teaching them about the history and struggle of Black people. When the residents first entered the program, they were first put on a three-month communication ban. Some of the residents were referred from the courts, and some were brought in by their parents or other organizations. The communication ban was designed to cut them off from outside negative influences. I think about a third of the residents were from other states. During the communication ban, they are required to write their autobiography and read *The Autobiography of Malcolm X* and *Manchild In A Promised Land*, and do a book report on each book. When I joined the staff, I added Carter D.Woodson's book. *The Mis-Education of the Negro*, and if they have not finished high school, they were required to attend GED preparation classes.

During this period, the residents were required to remain in the program for eighteen months. The program consisted of four phases. When the residents modified their behavior, they were moved to the next phase and they were given more responsibility. When they were promoted to the reentry phase of the program, they could work outside the facility. My first assignment was to do intake and case histories. The contract monitor taught me how to set up treatment plans. She was very helpful to me, and was very dedicated to the program. It took me about six months to learn the program. This was my first time working with drug abusers.

The program is actually run by the residents. I have always believed Black folks are a great people, but this was my first opportunity to experience the intellectual abilities of my people. There were about six or eight departments all run under the direction of the residents.

They had a front office coordinator who was responsible for the overall running of the program. When residents began to improve their behavior they were given an opportunity to head up a department.

The departments consisted of the front office coordinator, the education department, acquisition department, food services and the medical department. The residents prepared all the food. The organization had a few paid staff members. I was hired as a social worker. There were about five counselors. I had some concern about how the organization selected the counselors. Most of them were former residents and most of them were males. They didn't have any professional training, and they were too familiar with the resident's behavior. Most of them could not do one-on-one counseling sessions, or write the counseling notes.

A lot of good people passed through the doors, but they didn't last long, because the director ran the program like a dictator. He had a good relationship with few of the male staff members and sometimes with one or two females. However, it didn't last long with the females, especially if they took a strong position with him. There are several incidents that illustrate his attitude toward females that I will never forget.

We had a resident who had been in and out of the program several times. His name was Mark. He had a difficult time completing the program because he always began abusing drugs again. He finally finished the program. Mark was involved with a sister who had also finished the program. He was hired as a counselor. In my opinion, Mark had always been a "womanizer." He got Lisa pregnant. During Lisa's pregnancy, she found out she had cancer. In the meantime, Mark had started pursuing another resident who had recently entered the program. His behavior became so bad, the resident came to me and asked if I could make him leave her alone. Everybody in the environment knew about the situation. It was common gossip among the residents.

During this period, the director created a new program that was designed for mothers with children. Several sisters from out of state had their children with them. We had to set up separate facilities for them because children were not permitted to be housed in the same facility with adults. We also had some residents who were in the reentry phase of the program with children. They needed to start building a relationship with their children. The director put the program under my leadership. This was a difficult position for me.

After Lisa had her baby she remained in the facility. She didn't have any place to go. She didn't want to go back home because of the infestation of drugs in her neighborhood. I felt so sorry for Lisa. I can still feel her pain. She knew she was dying. I will never forget the one-on-one session with her after she was released from the hospital. She was suffering from nervous anxiety and depression because she didn't know what would happen to her baby. I felt helpless, I could not do anything for her.

One morning when I arrived at work, some of the residents met me at the door with bad news. Mark had attacked Lisa. I didn't want to believe it; Lisa had just recently been released from the hospital and was very weak. The director gave him a three-day suspension. He should have been fired. This is just an example of how females are treated in this male dominated society.

After the incident with Lisa, Ruthie, another sister who was a staff person, was beat to death by her spouse. Both sisters are now dead. Cancer eventually killed Lisa. I think she lived for about a year after the incident. I felt a little guilty about Ruthie's death because I knew she was being abused, but I didn't say anything because I didn't know her well enough. When I was first hired as staff member, Ruthie along with the director interviewed me for the job. Ruthie and I had a good relationship. Her office was located across the hall from my office. Every morning when I arrived at the office, I would go to her office to discuss the program, and sometimes we talked about this new man in her life. A few months later, I notice that Ruthie began to come to work with bandages on her foot, leg and face. When I inquired about her injuries, she would give me the usually excuses, "always an accident."

I believe the majority of women who are abused by their spouse are too ashamed to admit they are being abused, especially if they are still living with the abuser. When I look back, I believe I should have said something to her. When I went to view her body, she didn't look like a human being. Ruthie wrote beautiful poetry. She would often give me copies of her poems. And when she passed out the paychecks to the employees, she would always put one of her poems in the envelope. At that time I thought she wrote beautiful poetry. However, after her death, I started reading her poems again. I felt something in her poems that make me believe now, that she was a very sad and unhappy person. Her poems indicate that she foresaw her death. I think it is so sad that we live in a society where a woman has to pretend to be happy. I realize now that I never got to really know her. I just hope and pray that her spirit is at peace.

Whenever I hear Billy Holiday's songs, I get the feeling that she was also very unhappy. Even when Billy Holiday sang a song that was supposed to be a happy song, I could still feel the pain and sadness in her voice (I believe that is why I like gospel singing). I believe there are hidden messages in all songs and poetry that express the author's feelings and experiences at the time. However, I don't believe they are aware of what they are trying to say.

(Ruthie Jordan wrote the following poem on February 7, 1975)

I'LL SURVIVE

I remember the day we first met,
It seemed as if my eyes were covered with a net,
Something moved within me—but yet,
I couldn't take my eyes off you.
I knew then as I know now
That someday you would hurt me more
Than I've ever been hurt before.
But baby remember...

I have loved and loved again.
I have slept in the sun and shivered in the snow
Just waiting for someone to take away this emptiness.

I have been on a merry-go-round of life.
Growing dizzy with fear—as the music played on.
But I survived, I can still laugh and sing.
I can still love and that's what its all about.
I'm here, I'm alive, and I'll survive.

Each day it gets a little harder,
Everyday a burden, days are few—time is difficult
I'm waiting for the day when it's clearer—
The pain more bearable—
Time without you, what will it be?

Now along with the weather, I too, have grown cold
Why, because I've been alone—with no one to turn to.
Just sitting here worrying, anticipating,
Contemplating tomorrow.

But I survived, I can still laugh and sing.
I can still love and that's what it's all about.
I'm here, I'm love, and I'll survive.

I no longer have the warmth,
The comfort, the feeling of togetherness.
I need, oh how I need someone who will say—
You're not alone anymore.

But, I'll survive, I can still laugh and sing,
I can still love and that's what it's all about.
I'm here, I'm love, and I'll survive

I was not surprised when some of the sisters came to me and told me about the sexual demands made on them by the male staff members. It made me very angry, because most of these sisters had already experienced all kinds of abuse. They would beg me not to confront the counselor because they knew the counselor would retaliate against them by taking away their privileges. For example, they could take away their home visits or have them expelled from the program. I never had any problems with the residents, but the male staff members were dangerous to almost any female. They had big problems with me. For example, they had an acquisition department responsible for acquiring clothing, furniture, appliances, and other items the residents needed. I remember a donation from a men's clothing store. After the donation, I went to the department to see the donation; I didn't want to believe my eyes, the room was full of all kind of men's clothing, including leather coats and suits. The staff members removed the items they wanted before anything was given to the residents.

I think I had been with the program for about a year when I lost my brother. My mother had phoned me about him being hospitalized; I knew my brother was dying. When I met him in Indianapolis I knew he didn't have long to live. He passed away on May 4, 1985. I went home to attend his funeral. His death was very hard on my family, because it was the first death in my family since we lost my father. When I return to D.C. and went back to work, the director had hired a psychologist. I was glad to have Dr. Young on staff. Under her supervision, changes were implemented for conducting therapy sessions. Before her arrival, the residents would let off stream by calling each other derogatory names and using profanity.

Dr. Young eventually resigned due to male domination; she was not the type of woman to permit men to run over her. She had several confrontations with the director. One day she called me to her office and said she had some words with the director and asked him to leave her office. I hated to see her leave, because I learned a lot working with her. She did psychological evaluations of the residents, which helped me to setup the proper treatment plan. Unfortunately, I knew she wouldn't last long because the organization had a large turn-over of female employees. After she left everything went back to the former procedures. Although I had problems with the director and the male staff members, I was determined to stay with the organization. I felt the residents needed me and I was not ready to go back into a white controlled organization. Secondly, I had the opportunity to meet a lot of interesting people. The director invited a lot of people that were involved in the Black struggle to conduct seminars on site.

The only thing that helped me deal with the stressful situation was the trips I made to Africa. I went to Africa in 1985 and in 1986. There were a lot of things I didn't understand about the drug culture. Most of the staff members were former drug abuser. I had smoked marijuana and cigarettes, and I believe cigarettes are just as addictive as heroin or cocaine, but I had never used heroin or cocaine. Most of the staff members had been addicted to heroin, and some of them still exhibited "dope fiend behavior." Both staff and residents used this expression. It took me a long time to recognize this behavior; it is a strange kind of behavior. That's why I believe the staff and residents who had been addicted to drugs seem to understand each other; I often felted like an outsider because I had never been in the drug culture.

I think it was in 1986 or 87 when the organization lost the lease on the building. The director and the staff spent a lot of time trying to find another location. They tried to find a building in the city. They were unsuccessful because most people don't want to live next door to an organization that house drug abusers. I think it took about a year before they found another building. Mayor Marion Berry offered the director the Forest Haven Building, located in Laura, Maryland. The facility had been used to house teenagers with mental illnesses; there were several buildings on the site. It was during this period that I was going through a very stressful time with the director.

On moving day I became very sick (I have already talked about the day I came home from work and slept through a day I can't remember). I was in intensive care for several days. When I was discharged from the hospital and returned to work the organization had already moved to Laura. A few months before we moved to Forest Haven, the director hired Brother Bobby Dukes. We got off to a bad start. He later told me some of the staff told him he had to watch me because I had a bad attitude. We didn't get along at all. One day I saw him coming out of a building across the street from where I lived. We began to talk and he came up to my apartment. We had a long talk, and he told me how the male staff members had, "bad rap me." He said they had problems with me because I was always confronting them about the sisters. He said it took a while before he realized what I was trying to do. He said he later learned to admire me because I wouldn't let the male staff members run over me. Bobby said they would often say, "Sister Rasheedah needs a man," when they had discussions about me. That is the attitude of some Black men if they don't see you involved with a man. They feel that something has to be wrong with you or they will call you a lesbian. Bobby and I had a good relationship until his death. When he passed from this world, I grieved for the brother because I really cared for him.

MY FRIST TRIP TO THE CARIBBEAN ISLANDS

In 1987 I made two trips out of the country; I went to Africa and Jamaica. This was my first trip to the Caribbean Islands. When I worked for OEO (Office of Economic Opportunity), several sisters in my office used to go to the islands seeking male companionship. When they returned to the States, they appeared to be excited about their experience. But I have never been impressed with the idea of spending money seeking male companionship. The organization founded by Marcus Garvey (UNITA), was organizing a trip to Jamaica for the celebration of his one-hundredth birthday; that was my only reason for going to Jamaica. I admired the teachings of Marcus Garvey. I enjoyed my trip because it gave me the opportunity to visit the place of his birth and witness the Jamaican people celebrating his one-hundredth birthday. I also went to Libya that same year.

When I returned to work, the director had hired Sister Zelpah for the position of contract monitor. She was already working in the director's office. Sister Zelpah and I had a very good relationship. We became good friends. She was a member of the Hebrew Israelites who lived in Damona Israel. Sister Zelpah is the most spiritual individual I have ever met, especially in this country. She was very helpful to me. She always kept me informed about the viciousness of the male staff members and why she felt they had a problem with me. Black men in this country resent being confronted by women, especially Black women. It's an insult to their male ego. It didn't prevent me from confronting them on issues of disagreement.

Sister Zelpah eventually resigned and moved back to Israel. It was about this time, in 1988, that I decided to travel to Egypt. I became interested in traveling to Egypt when I heard Tony Browder talk about taking a group there. I had always wanted to go to Egypt and had tried on several occasions to get a visa to travel there. It is very difficult for women to get a visa to travel alone to some Middle Eastern countries (I have already discussed my trip to Egypt). When I returned to this country and went back to work, I went to my office and discovered they had given my office to a new employee who had been hired as an aide counselor. That didn't bother me too much. However, when I inquired about the whereabouts of my office, no one could tell me anything.

Some of the residents came to me and said they would show me where I could find my things. They had taken my things and thrown them in the corner of a big room. I had never before felt the pain I felt at that time. I don't understand my frame of mind at that time because I should have resigned, but for some reason, I was determined to remain with the organization. I didn't have any problem with money because I had enough money in my savings account to last me for a couple of years. At that time, my sister was still living. She tried her best to get me to resign. I think what bothered me so much was the fact that this treatment was coming from Black folks. I now believe that a large number of Black folks in this country need to be in treatment. Slavery did a very good job on the mental state of Black Americans; I call it "slavery mentality." We still have a lot of Black folks hurting each other because we have been taught to hate ourselves.

I asked for a new location for my office but my requests was denied. The residents helped me to set up my office in the big room. I didn't have a private place to interview the residents because there were other people working in the room. I resolved the problem by taking my clients to the library or conference room. I think it was in 1989 or 1990 when the director hired an administrative manager. She had very good administrative skills but she didn't have any people skills. From the first day she came to work, she exhibited a negative attitude toward me. I knew what the director and the staff had told her about me, and it wasn't good. Our relationship grew worse everyday. I think it was about this time that she convinced the director to fire me. Even today, I don't know why I was fired. I think I was off from work for about six months, when I went to see some of the residents' graduate from the program. The director saw me and he asked me to come back to work. I didn't feel too bad about being off work because I needed the rest. I went back to work and everything was the same. They gave me a new office and a raise.

In 1990, my sister's husband had a heart attack. I think he had a second heart attack in June or July of the same year. I think it may have been caused from the stress of trying to buy a house. Their landlord had sold the house they were living in and had given them an eviction notice; they had to move within a couple of months. They were trying to find a house to rent or buy. They eventually found a house to buy. After they completed the process of buying the house, I went to see it and that is when I noticed that my sister had lost a lot of weight. I knew she was worried about her husband's health. They had a very close relationship. One day she came to visit me; in the process of trying to sit down, she fell off the chair. At that time I knew my sister was real sick. About a week later she went into the hospital and was told she had liver cancer. I knew my sister was dying. This was a difficult time for me. My sister and I were very close. Although the organization knew my sister was seriously ill, they continued to give me memos each time I had to take off due to her illness. My sister died January 1,1991 and her husband died about nine months later. (I have already discussed the death of my sister.)

MY MOTHER BECAME VERY ILL

The next couple of years several things happened, one thing was that my mother became very ill. I think it was the latter part of 1992. I knew something was wrong because my mother had phoned me several times asking me to send her money. I didn't understand what was happening because my mother had enough income to take care of her financial needs. I later discovered she was trying to take care of Chris, my youngest brother and Bill, my nephew. They were still living with her. My niece told me that my mother had started acting strange. At that time, my mother was about 87 years old. My brothers said my mother had started complaining about being sick and would continually ask them to take her to the emergency room. The doctors couldn't find anything wrong with her; they said my mother was still grieving my sister's death.

A few months later she went into the hospital and I took off work and went to Anniston. When I went to the hospital and talked to the doctors they said she had a bowel obstruction and they had to operate on her. After the operation, my mother was healing well but she refused to speak to me. I tried everything to get her to speak to me. Nevertheless, she refused to say anything. My brother said my mother was waiting for my niece, Geraldine, to come and see her. My niece had always been my mother's favorite. We have always believed my mother loved my niece more than she loved any of her children.

I realized my mother didn't want to see me. She was waiting for my niece. It hurt me when my mother wouldn't communicate with me, but I could also understand how she felt about my niece. I accepted the reality that this child had played the role of a daughter when my sister and I were no longer at home.

After I returned to D.C., I phoned Geraldine and begged her to visit my mother. She said her husband wouldn't permit her to travel because she was pregnant and he feared she might lose her baby. My niece was married to a soldier and she traveled with him during this period. My youngest brother, Christopher, and my nephew, Bill, were both heavy drinkers.

When my mother was released from the hospital, I was deeply concerned about her, but I felt there were enough people to adequately take care of her. My brother Willie and his wife had two adult daughters living in Anniston and Willie and his wife lived only a block from her house. I didn't see any reason for me to go to Anniston to care for her.

My brother felt I should be the one to take care of her, but I refused to take on that responsibility. They did everything they could to try to make me feel guilty for not coming south to care for her. They would often phone me and say my mother needed a female to care for her. I knew she didn't want me to care for her. She really wanted my niece to care for her. Our relationship had never been good, and I knew she would destroy me if I had to be with her on a daily basis. My mother died November 19, 1993. When I went home for her funeral, my brothers jumped all over me especially the two alcoholics living in the home. That is when I realized my mother had died because she was tired of living. I was there for only a few days and they almost drove me crazy. They were drunk almost every day. I can't imagine what they did to her, especially at her age.

When I was trying to make arrangements for her funeral and burial, they would give a lot of advice and not one penny toward expenses. By the time I returned to D.C., I was a nervous wreck. The day before my mother's funeral, my brother, Willie, and Bill, my nephew, had an altercation. The night before I left for D.C., my brother Chris and Bill got in a physical fight. I was just glad to get back to D.C. in one piece. My niece Geraldine came to mother's funeral. She was fainting and falling out from guilt. My mother had a will. She left the house and everything to my niece. That didn't bother me too much. However, my niece and brother, Chris, had a very bad relationship. My niece, nephew, and my youngest brother were raised up together. Chris resented my niece because he knew my mother favored Geraldine over him and he was very angry when he found out my mother had left my niece in charge of everything. My niece wanted to put Chris out of the house and sell it. She hired a lawyer. My name was also on the will.

When I returned to D.C., I consulted my lawyer in Detroit. He said my niece could not sell the house without my signature. He also told me my mother didn't have the authority to will the house to my niece when she and my father still had children living, and I was my family's oldest living child. I had paid the last taxes on the property. I knew I would never live in the house and left it up to him to save the house. I told Chris that I would support him but I was not going to fight with my niece about a house. My niece took all the furniture she had bought for my mother. My brothers still feel I should have taken care of my mother but I feel I did the right thing for me. I believe even today my mother willed herself to die. I think she was tired of Chris and Bill and just gave up.

During the period after the death of my mother, I was going through so much turmoil on the job; I am surprised I was able to function from one day to the next. As soon as I returned to work, the administrative manager gave me a memo for being off to attend my mother's funeral. The organization hired a new counselor. He was from California and had previously been in treatment at Synanon, a therapeutic program in California. He later became a counselor. He eventually moved his family to D.C. I liked the brother and we had a warm relationship. He was a good counselor. He only had one problem, he could not write counselor notes. During that period the contract was demanding that the counselors do more than just talk and counsel the residents. They were requested to keep records of all contact with residents and write the counseling notes. I think he had been with the organization for about a year when they started asking him to write counselor notes on his one-on-one sessions.

He had no idea how to write counseling notes. They asked me to teach him how to write his notes. He started coming to my office daily and we would spend about an hour a day. After about a month, I started checking his case folders. I discovered he could barely write one line about his contact with the residents. At that time, I discovered I would have a difficult time trying to teach him how to write his notes. One day he came to my office and said to me, "Sister Rasheedah I am going to be honest with you, I am forty six years old and I started abusing drugs as a teenager and don't have any formal education." He could read and communicate what he read, but he could not transfer it to writing.

I realized at that time he would need professional help. I continued to try to help him, but frankly, I was not in the state of mind to give him adequate help. He was also having problems with the organization. They were putting pressure on him. I felt sorry for him but there was very little I could do to help him. During this period, he didn't live too far from my house and the days when he drove his car, he would give me a ride to and from work. He had a car and two motorcycles. I only rode with him when he was driving his car. On the days that he rode his motorcycle, he would phone me in time for me to catch a ride with the organization's van. At that time the organization's main office was located in D.C. The facility for the treatment program was located in Laurel, Maryland about thirty miles from D.C. He loved his motorcycles. He often talked about how he loved riding his motorcycles in the hills in California.

AN INCIDENT I CAN NEVER FORGET

This next incident will always remain with me. I think it was on a Friday night, And both Brother Kaira and I were working the late shift. Earlier that night he showed me a memo he had received from the organization. He was despondent and angry because he felt the organization wasn't giving him enough time to learn how to write his notes. I asked him what was he going to do about the memo he received. He asked me if I would help him write a response to the memo, I told him, I would be glad to help him. That night as we were getting ready to leave for home, I was in the front office waiting for a driver for the van and he went to get his motorcycle.

We all left the facility at the same time. He was in front of us (the van). We had been on the expressway for about fifteen minutes when suddenly I noticed from the other side of the expressway a car had crossed over and was coming directly in front of us. The car hit the motorcycle and I saw Brother Kaira go up in the air and the motorcycle went another way. The resident stopped the van so suddenly I fell on the floor, that is the first time I witnessed this kind of accident. We got out of the van and had to look for Brother Kaira. We found him lying on the side of the expressway. I ran over to help him. I felt for life signs; there were no life signs. That is when I knew he was dead. This happened on May 24, 1994.

I remember seeing the driver get in the car with some other people, and they just drove off. We waited for the medical unit to pick up his body. We went back to the facility to phone the director about the accident. I will never understand how this brother who hit the motorcycle could just walk off after taking a life.

MY RELATIONSHIP WITH
THE DIRECTOR GREW WORSE

After the death of Brother Kaira, my relationship with the director grew worse. I think it was sometime in 1993 when my supervisor left the country. The director placed me under the supervision of James, a former resident. James had completed the program, and had been moved to a staff position (counselor). I didn't want to believe the director would sink this low. I believe he did it to humiliate me. James wasn't even a good counselor. My previous supervisor had asked me to teach James how to write his counselor notes. When I tried to train him most of the time he didn't understand me. He was a high school dropout who had spent all of his time in the drug culture. I tried to work with James. However, it was almost impossible because he still exhibited dope fiend behavior. I think I had been working under James' supervision about six months when I had to make a trip to Detroit. I met all the requirements to get the time off, made plane reservations and was planning to leave on a Sunday. During this period, the agency had a policy that only one staff person worked on the weekend.

The following Thursday was supposed to be my last workday. James approached me and asked me to work on Sunday, the day I was scheduled to leave. I told him I would not change my reservations because I had an appointment to see my lawyer on Monday. He said he could not find anyone else to work that day. James had very poor supervision skills because a good supervisor would never sign a leave slip without first making arrangements to replace the employee on Friday. The director's secretary phoned me with a message. It said that if I didn't work on Sunday, I was not to return to the agency (I was fired). That was in 1994. After I returned to D.C., I never went back. About a year later, a staff person told me James had gone back to abusing drugs. I saw him a few years ago; he was back in treatment and had had a couple of heart attacks. I really felt sorry for him.

I DECIDED TO RETIRE

I was sixty-two years old when I stopped working. I was tired and didn't feel like working any more. I didn't have any idea what I was going to do. The organization did not have a retirement plan, so I applied for my social security benefits. I left the organization in June of 1994. I was with the organization for ten years. I was glad I had reached the age where I could stop working. Since the organization didn't have a retirement plan, social security benefits were my only income and it was very small. I have learned to live with less income. I had a small saving account, but I knew it wouldn't last long. I still had a strong desire to live in Africa. I knew I could live comfortably in Africa on my social security benefits. I made two trips to Africa in 1995. During my first trip I got sick and had to return to this country. I arrived home about a week before the Million-Man March. At that time, I had not been diagnosed with emphysema.

I think I had been home about a week when I got a phone call from my friend Edward Vaughn. He and some friends would be attending the Million-Man March and they would be driving from Detroit. They wanted to rest at my house before going to the march. Although I was still sick, I couldn't refuse my friend the use of my home. On the day of the march, they arrived in D.C. about 4:00 a.m. He brought three brothers with him. My apartment is small and I didn't have enough sleeping room. Some of them slept on the floor and made the best of the situation.

I didn't attend the march, but I witnessed this historical event on TV. I had never witnessed anything like it. There was a spirit in this country that I had never experienced before. The faces of this sea of a million beautiful black men shook the world. For the first time in my life, I felt there was real hope for my people. In addition, I believed this event caught the government and the news media off guard. They didn't want to believe Minister Farrakhan could bring this many Black men together. Since I am on the subject of Minister Farrakhan, in my opinion, I believe he is the only Black man living today who is teaching the truth about the condition of Blacks and he is not afraid to speak out. He has taken a positive position for the role of women.

Before I end *My Life-Story*, I want to do a tribute to my mother. I have tried to be honest about my relationship with my mother. Some of it was my fault and some of it is the result of my mother's cultural background. I wished we could have had a good "mother and daughter relationship," but that didn't happen. I needed her to show me love. I now believe she loved me; she just didn't know how to show it. I believe a mother's love is the greatest force on earth. I think it is of the utmost importance for us to keep in mind that we all came from a cultural background of slavery. Although we don't wear the shackles or chains, psychological damage has been done. When I try to make sense of my relationship with my mother, I have to go back to something my father said to me years ago. I was home visiting my family when I had a confrontation with my mother. She made me so angry I started packing my bags to leave for home. My father was sitting in the living room. After I finished my packing, I went back to the living room. I noticed my father had tears in his eyes. He said to me, "Lorine I am going to tell you why you and your mother don't get along. You are just like your mother." I didn't want to believe him. However, since I have grown older, I believe he was right because I see myself exhibiting some of the same characteristics as my mother. My mother was the strongest woman I have ever known. I remember several incidents that have led me to this conclusion. When I was a child, all the Black women had their babies at home. There was this family who lived directly across the street from us. I remember playing in the front yard when the young women were in labor, I could hear them hollering and crying. I was too young to understand what was happening. However, I remember the times when mother went into labor, and we would be in the next room, but we never heard my mother cry out. We first knew there was a new baby when we heard the baby cry. I remember asking my mother why she never cried out. She said crying wouldn't stop the pain.

There is another incident that I remember all too well. It happened during the Civil Rights Movement. I can't remember the year but I think it was in 1965 or 1966. I was involved with some young radicals who were trying to integrate the bus station. During this period, I would fly from Detroit to Birmingham. I had to ride a bus from Birmingham to Anniston. I was determined not to ride or sit in the Jim Crow section of the bus station. I think I spent about a week with my family. When I got ready to leave I explained to my father and mother what I was trying to do. They were concerned about my welfare but they never tried to interfere with my decision I made.

My father said mother would go to the bus station with me. I was afraid for my mother but it didn't seem to bother her. When we arrived at the bus station, we went to the side where it said whites only. I was so scared I was shaking. I was more afraid for my mother than for myself. The bus station was full of white folks they didn't seem to pay us too much attention. I was so scared. I went to get coffee from the machine. When I returned to my seat, I didn't see my mother. A white woman told me my mother was in the bathroom. When I went into the bathroom, my mother was in a conversation with two white women. My mother asked me why was I looking for her. I remember telling my mother I was very worried about her. She said, "I don't need you to worry about me, I can take care of you and me." My mother did not exhibit any fear. When I look back at that time, I realize my mother was a very strong woman. I believe my father recognized her strength and that is why he had so much respect for her. It didn't matter what my mother did, I never heard my father speak out against her. I never heard my father curse at my mother. When they had a disagreement, my mother would lead the argument and my father would say very little. I remember how we used to tease my father because he would always give his paycheck to my mother. I realize now my father gave his paycheck to my mother because he had faith in her and he knew she would do the right thing with it. When I look back at my relationship with my mother, I feel sometimes it wasn't very good but I am glad she was in my life. I know all my strength came from her.

I WANT TO PAY TRIBUTE TO OTHER WOMEN I ADMIRE AND RESPECT

While I am on the subject of strong women, I want to also pay tribute to other women whom I admire and respect. I have a lot of respect for Angela Davis. I have had the opportunity to meet her and hear her speak on several occasions. I believe she is one of the most brilliant Black women in this country. I remember the time when Angela Davis was jailed because of her involvement with the Soledad Brothers. I believe she was accused of supplying guns to the Soledad Brothers when they had a shootout. I believe a judge was killed. I attended several rallies for her. Because of her affiliation with the Communist party, a lot of Black folks didn't support her.

I read the "Cress Theory," years ago. When I lived in Detroit, I had the opportunity to learn more about Dr. Welsing because she lived in the D.C. area and her office was located in D.C. I have heard her speak and have read several of her books. I always felt a sense of honor just to be in the presence of these great women.

Another woman I have deep respect for is Fannie Lou Hamer. I didn't have the opportunity to meet her, but I can remember the role she played during the 1964 Democratic National Convention and I had a chance to hear her speak. I will never forget her talking about what happened to her when she was returning from participating in a voter registration drive. She was arrested in Mississippi and had to spend time in a Mississippi jail. She talked about how they made the inmates use their blackjacks on her. She said the inmates told her to lie down on the bed. She said that every time they hit her, her legs would draw up. One of the inmates would hold her legs while the other inmate beat her. She said the inmates beat her until she passed out. She said for weeks after the incident she couldn't sleep on her back. When she was discussing the beating, I could feel her pain. She also said she was still suffering from a permanent kidney injury and a blood clot in her left eye. I believe that her early death is the result of that beating because it was too late for her to get adequate medical treatment for the beating. There have been a lot of Black women who have suffered trying to make life better for their people.

I admire Anita Hill; I didn't know much about her. When I saw her testify against the confirmation of Carence Thomas for the Supreme Court, I actually cried for the sister, because she had to be a strong woman to sit before that body of White racist Senators, and be ridiculed before the nation. Black folks, especially Black men, also attacked her. I felt that in my heart she was telling the truth. We now have a Black Supreme Court Judge who has so much self-hate and hate for Black folks he will never vote for anything to benefit Black folks. He has always voted with the conservative judges. In my opinion the word "conservative," is just a code word for white supremacy. I have never understood how a Black American could call himself or herself a "conservative," because the only thing we have to conserve is slavery. Some people have problems understanding the kind of harassment Black and White women had to tolerate in the work place. On some of my jobs, I often had to fight off Black and White men.

WRITING MY LIFE STORY

Today's date is January 17, 2003—my Birthday. This is the first time I have worked on *My Life Story* in about three or four months. I am not sure what happened but I got tired of it. On December 19, 2002, I got sick and spent ten days in the hospital. My neighbor had to call 911 because I had a temperature of 103. 1 made myself a promise that when I came home I would finish *My Life Story*. I had a very bad experience in the hospital.

When I first start writing *My Life Story*. I didn't think about getting it published. However, after several of my friends read some excerpts, they convinced me it was good enough to be published. One day when I was listening to the radio, I heard a sister discussing a book she had published. This book was published several years ago. I have read the book and considered her a good writer. She had opened a publishing company where she would help you publish your book. I got the Information off the Internet and wrote her. She phoned me and I told her I wanted her to evaluate *My Life Story* for publication. I mailed her the fee and a few pages of *My Life Story*. When the pages were returned to me, she had crossed out all the commentary. She said she crossed it out because it didn't have anything to do with my life. I felt she was not in the position to tell me what to say about my life.

I am not a writer but this is my life story and I have the right to express my opinion on any issue I want to. If I can't get it published with my commentary, then it won't be published. I don't want anyone to read *My Life Story* just to learn about me. I want them to learn about the Black experience and what has happened to Black folks during my lifetime, and our struggle to survive. I realize there has been a lot of progress for some Black folks, but the masses of our people still suffer from high unemployment, homelessness, poor health care and crime. If we look at the number of Black men in prisons, you would think Black men are the only people who commit crimes in this country; Black men are the majority on death row.

I also want to mention another brother, Mumia Abu-Jamal. He had been a member of the Black Panther party and was a supporter of the Move Organization. He has been on death row for almost twenty years. I believe he is one of the strongest brothers alive today. A policeman shot him in December of 1981. He was driving a cab and came upon a street where the police were beating his brother. A confrontation broke out and the police beat him. A policeman was also shot and killed. Eyewitnesses saw one or more men running from the scene. Abu-Jamal Mumia was beaten so badly the doctors didn't expect him to live. I don't believe he received a fair trial and he had one of the worse judges in the state. Amnesty International called for a new trial for Abu-Jamal Mumia, but the request had been denied.

I stopped writing on *My Life Story* in November of 2002. I didn't understand why. The only answer I could come up with didn't make sense. I believe that it was about the time the Bush administration started their propaganda about attacking Iraq. This is the kind of behavior that worries me. I think what really bothers me is the attitude of the American people.

The American people are living in fear, and the Bush Administration is using this fear to beat the drums for war. This kind of arrogance is what worries me. Eleven years ago there was the Gulf War that killed thousand of innocent people, and the ten years of economic sanctions has killed about 500,000 Iraq children. Presently, there are more than 500,000 Iraq children still suffering from malnutrition. The economic sanctions have created all kinds of health problems. For example, after twelve years of bombing, the United States has destroyed Iraq water systems and has banned such items as chlorine so they can't purify drinking water.

The majority of the Iraqi people don't have clean water. I believe this is " a crime against humanity." Iraq has been brutalized, terrorized, and brought to its knees, and yet the Bush administration is telling the American public Iraq is a security threat. There has not been a war fought in this county since the Civil War, and they don't have any idea what a war can do to a country. We have not suffered mega-ton, uranium-depleted bombs falling on us. Iraq has a population of about 22 million people and they have already lost about 2 million people from the Gulf War and the war with Iran, and most of the people are dependent on food distribution by the Iraq Government.

Mandela said the Bush Administration is going to create a "global holocaust" in the Middle East. Since the begining of 2003, this government has sent more than 100,000 Troops to Iraq (in Kuwait), the biggest buildup since the Gulf War. This was done for the sold purpose of taking control of Iraq oil. They are even talking about the use of nuclear weapons. What really makes me sad is that the mainstream news media is helping the Bush Administration carry out the worse kind of psychological warfare. I am 72 years old and I have never witnessed before what I see happening today. There is a diabolical force that is so strong in this country today, that I often have to turn the TV off during the news programs, because it almost makes me physically sick to hear the lies and distortions that are being feed to the public.

On February 22, 2003, protest marches were held throughout the world. They estimated two million marched in London; about three million in Rome, about 75,000 in New York and that doesn't include the demonstrations in 600 small cities around the world. I think I read somewhere that Bush said he believes in a divine force that shapes human destiny. I think he should look closely at what has happened in the past few years. First the shuttle "Columbia," blew up and killed seven astronauts. Second, in Chicago, twenty-one people were killed and fifty-seven injured in a nightclub stampede. A fire broke out in a nightclub in Rhode Island where about one hundred people were killed and about one hundred fifty more were injured. The day after the largest demonstration in the history of the world, we had the worse snowstorm in decades, the largest accumulation of snow since the snow blizzard of 1892. I have been in DC for almost twenty years and I have never seen this much snow before. The snowstorm shut the city down. When we go to bed thinking we are safe, there is a divine force that reminds us there is a power that can take control.

We are presently experiencing all kinds of tragic events. Everything is out of natural order, there is a dark cloud hanging over this country unlike anything I have ever witnessed in my lifetime. I believe we have a mad man in the White House and most of his people are so far to the right they don't even know if they have a left hand. Some people are afraid of this administration. I have heard some White folks say they believe if the war is going on by the next election, and the President finds himself losing the election, he might suspend the Constitution and declare himself president for another term. After what happened in the last election, I believe anything can happen. I believe there was a coup de'-tat from the last election. I don't believe anyone will admit to it. Most people would rather say, "President Bush stole the election," yet this government has the nerve to talk about fair elections in other countries. That is why other people in other countries hate this government.

I BELIEVE TUPASC SHAKUR WAS AN "OLD SPIRIT"

Before I end *My Life Story*, there is another individual I will discuss, Tupac Shakur, although I didn't listen to his rap. When I first heard this kind of music, I didn't like it. There was something about the music I couldn't understand. I didn't like it because the lyrics were insulting to Black women. However, after the death of Tupac, I felt sorry for his mother. One day I was in a bookstore and noticed a book entitled "Tupac Shakur," I bought the book. After reading the book, I went out and rented some of his movies. Though I still have not heard any of his rap music, I have come to believe that he is an "old spirit." I will discuss this more at the end of *My Life Story*.

THE RAPPERS ARE ANGRY AND WHO IS TO BLAME

I believe some of our young rappers are very angry. They are expressing this anger in the lyrics of their songs. When I first heard the rappers, I found myself repeating the same words and expressing the same attitude of some older Black folks. I believe now some of our young rappers have a right to be angry because we didn't do anything to protect them after the so-called Civil Rights Movement. Some Black folks felt they had made it over, and all they wanted was a piece of American apple pie. We didn't take the time to teach them anything. We left the sisters behind. They couldn't find husbands. They followed the course of nature and had babies without husbands. We also turned our children over to this racist society, and they couldn't adjust to it. A capitalist system is about making money and our young men and women found a way to use their artistic talents to make money, so they began to use words and sounds to express themselves. They didn't have any help or anyone to guide them. Black folks just stood around ridiculing them; we didn't rally around our young people. That is why, in the past, we have lost so many of our artists.

I believe Michael Jackson is one of the greatest entertainers in the history of this country, and we are presently helping this white racist society destroy him. I have heard Black folks ridicule him worse than the white news media. I have often read in the newspapers where they call him weird and other derogatory names and it is very sad when I hear how they make fun of him on TV. It doesn't matter to me if he wanted to be white, brown or black. Michael Jackson is still our child and when he is attacked by the news media, they are attacking all of us. Frankly speaking, I have witnessed many more weird white artists than Black artists. I believe Michael Jackson is an "old spirit." I also believe Shango, Murnia, and Ruth Jordan are "old spirits."

MY INTERPRETATION OF SPIRITUALITY

I want to bring *My Life Story* to an end by discussing my interpretation of spirituality. I understand I will be criticized, but at my age, I don't have the time to worry about criticism. I believe there are two types of people on earth, spiritual individuals and unspiritual individuals. Most people have difficulties understanding spiritual individuals. They will call them crazy, weird, and strange. According to the teaching of all religious books, the spirit (soul) is eternal and when the body dies the spirit goes either to Heaven or Hell. I don't accept this concept. This teaching is especially relevant to most Black folks because the majority have been indoctrinated in the teaching of the Bible, and some of our people refuse to study any other religious doctrine. Because we have suffered so much during our lifetime on Earth, it is easy to believe that there will be a better life for us when we leave this Earth. When we listen to the songs and prayers of Black folks, they talk about how they will walk the streets of gold, fly around heaven, drink milk and honey, and those who have committed sins will burn in hell. And the classification of sin is breaking the Ten Commandments.

Many Black folks believed religion was a gift from the White man. White supremacy is so intertwined in the teaching of religion; it has been virtually impossible for Black folks to understand spirituality. It doesn't have anything to do with the manner in which an individual chooses to worship. I believe when an individual dies, the spirit (soul) leaves the body only for a short period of time or takes a long rest. In our lifetime on earth, we cannot do everything we are required to do. Our spirit has a special mission, and there are many missions to complete. And our mission is to make this a better world for everyone. If the spirit (soul) is eternal, then it must return to Earth to fulfill these missions. In most cases, we don't understand our mission. Sometimes the human mind covers up the divine purpose of the spirit because we are too busy trying to satisfy the desires of the body.

We live in a capitalistic society where more attention is paid to the outer life. We are taught to believe materialistic things will make us happy. Presently we find some of our people spending more time shopping for things, or we will hold on to houses, cars, boats and other possessions because we believe these thing will make us happy. There is nothing wrong with material things, but, they are just "things." In some cases, we will hold on to lovers and family members because we depend on them to make us happy. In some cases, they can become possessions and we want to dominate them as if we own them. And when we lose them (they die), we have difficulties giving them up. We must understand that death is not the end. It is the beginning of another stage of our evolution.

We are eternal travelers and we have to continue our journey until we reach our goal. And our goal is perfection. We cannot reach perfection in an imperfect world. America is an unnatural environment because she is corrupt. The federal government and the Church are corrupt. It is impossible for the American people to become spiritual individuals when the Church and the government do everything to keep the masses ignorant. The Creator made the Earth and human beings to be perfect. Although the Creator knew that some human beings (the Devil), would try to destroy the Earth. This is why some human beings must return to Earth to complete the cycle of making this a perfect world. The world has existed for billions of years and will continue to exist until in some distant future, paradise is established on Earth. The Earth will be the final Heaven, not some distant place in the sky.

We are obligated to work for righteousness until we create a perfect world. That is why we must begin to look at ourselves as spiritual beings, and not get caught up in the dogmatism of religion. Men wrote all the religious books, and they are unacceptable to me because man has not reached perfection. Everything the Supreme power created is in natural order. If man had created the sun and moon, they would have burned up millions of years ago. The above analysis is why I believe Michael Jackson, Tupac Shakur, Billy Holiday and many other great folks are "old spirits." I believe Tupac and Billy Holiday may have already returned to Earth in their new lives, though they may not be in the entertainment business. Most of us will never know because we have been led to believe that death is the end. I believe Malcolm X, Fannie Lou Hamer, and Paul Robson were all "old spirits." Paul Robson was one of the greatest men this country has ever produced, Black or white. Yet very few Black people know anything about him, and how he fought for the liberation of Black folks and the White working class. You don't hear anyone talking about him because the government labeled him "a Communist." To prevent him from traveling out of the country, they took his passport.

COMING TO A CLOSE

I am going to bring my autobiography to a close. I truly believe that we will not make any real progress in this country until we change our behavior. First, we must know ourselves, and the historical events about Black people before and after slavery. Second, we must reeducate our children; the schools will never teach our children about the history of Black folks, we must teach them at home. I just hope anyone who read about my life will learn something about the struggle of Black folks in this country, especially Black women. I am thankful to my Creator that I have lived to reach the age of seventy-two.

I leave you love, I leave you hope, I leave you a thirst for knowledge. I leave you self-determination, I leave you courage to protect and to educate our young people, I leave you the will to trust and to believe in yourself and in your own people, I leave you faith, I leave you the desire to live harmoniously with all people, I leave you the responsibility of being your brother's keeper. And finally, I leave you vision to see yourself for who the Creator has made you to be and not what the White man and others say that you are.

BOOK AVAILABLE THROUGH

Milligan Books, Inc.

If The Sun, Moon and Stars Could Talk $12.00

Order Form

Milligan Books, Inc.

1425 W. Manchester Ave., Suite C, Los Angeles, CA 90047

(323) 750-3592

Name________________________________ Date __________

Address____

City_____________________ State_____ Zip Code ______

Day Telephone _____________________________________

Evening Telephone__________________________________

Book Title____

Number of books ordered___ Total ....$ ___________

Sales Taxes (CA Add 8.25%) ....$ ___________

Shipping & Handling $4.90 for one book ..$ ___________

Add $1.00 for each additional book...........$ ___________

Total Amount Due....................................$ ___________

☐ Check ☐ Money Order ☐ Other Cards ___________

☐ Visa   ☐ MasterCard Expiration Date ___________

Credit Card No. ____________________________________

Driver License No. __________________________________

Make check payable to Milligan Books, Inc.

_______________________   _______________________

Signature   Date

9 780097 646901